"This is a fascinating accoun[] modern behavioral analysis. [This book will get you thinking] about yourself, your partner, and love in ways that you probably haven't thought of before. It brings scientific illumination to the candle lights of intimacy."

—**Andrew Christensen, PhD,** is professor of psychology at UCLA, a cofounder of integrative behavioral couple therapy, and author of *Reconcilable Differences*

For Bruna,

Colleague and Friend

-Christopher...

ACT & RFT *in* RELATIONSHIPS

Helping Clients Deepen Intimacy *and* Maintain Healthy Commitments Using Acceptance *and* Commitment Therapy *and* Relational Frame Theory

JOANNE DAHL, PHD
IAN STEWART, PHD
CHRISTOPHER MARTELL, PHD
JONATHAN S. KAPLAN, PHD

CONTEXT PRESS
An Imprint of New Harbinger Publications, Inc.

Publisher's Note

Distributed in Canada by Raincoast Books

Copyright © 2013 by JoAnne Dahl, Ian Stewart,
      Jonathan Kaplan, & Christopher Martell
     . New Harbinger Publications, Inc.
      5674 Shattuck Avenue
      Oakland, CA 94609
      www.newharbinger.com

Cover design by Amy Shoup
Acquired by Melissa Kirk
Edited by Will DeRooy

Library of Congress Cataloging in Publication Data on file

Printed in the United States of America

FSC
www.fsc.org
MIX
Paper from responsible sources
FSC® C011935

15 14 13

10 9 8 7 6 5 4 3 2 1   First printing

Contents

Foreword

Dear reader,

About twice a year, my husband and I take a long road trip to visit my brothers and their families. They always take the time to spruce up the guest room and light a candle for our arrival. After the fun of greeting everyone, my husband and I move our suitcases into the guest room. Each time, as I swing the door open, I am greeted with a warm and welcoming sign that hangs right above the bed: "If there is anything better than to be loved, it is to be loving." The sign is plain and unpretentious—simple white letters on a dark background, signed by no one. Yet its message settles in easily, like gentle snow falling on the winter ground. Creating the stuff of this message in your clinical work—to *be* loving is what this book is about.

As coauthor of *The Mindful Couple: How Acceptance and Mindfulness Can Lead You to the Love You Want*, as well as a longtime practitioner and trainer of acceptance and commitment therapy (ACT) and a participant in the ACT and relational frame theory (RFT) community, I am delighted to introduce this coherent and thoughtful book that marries behavior analytic science and love. The authors provide the reader with a way forward in the challenging yet fulfilling enter- prise of couples and relationship counseling.

I first met JoAnne Dahl in mid-2004 at an Association for Contextual and Behavioral Science conference. She immediately struck me as someone whose work was grounded in compassion and primarily concerned with the "ways" of love and relationship. But she also struck me as a person interested in science's role in these matters, working seriously to develop relevant clinical knowledge through her position as associate professor in the department of psychology at the University of Uppsala in Sweden.

And she has joined others of similar character to write this book. One of them is Ian Stewart, a faculty member in the psychology department at the National University of Ireland, Galway and a longtime associate and friend, as well as a brilliant researcher who has brought his talents in understanding relational frame theory to this endeavor. There are many times when I have been truly grateful for his diligence in helping others to understand the RFT analysis of human language.

Christopher R. Martell, a professor at the University of Washington in Seattle, brings fundamental knowledge to this book with his expertise in behavioral activation. He is an expert in this intervention, training people to embolden themselves by taking action linked to values.

And last but surely not least is author Jonathan S. Kaplan, a clinician and adjunct professor who writes and shares his important work on television and radio, and has been featured in O, The Oprah Magazine as well as on BBC News and MSNBC. He is invested in cultivating peace, purpose, and presence through his work—a fitting way to round out the contributions to and development of this book.

While reading *ACT and RFT in Relationships*, I regularly returned to and considered the notion of intimacy. The word itself is related to the word *familiar*, meaning "well-known." Finding a way to be well-known in a relationship, with all of the fear, dread, and secrets that can accompany this—as well as the promise—is a unique challenge for human beings. It is often difficult for us to be fully present to our own emotional experience, let alone to open ourselves up and share that experience with another. Indeed, the prospect of being well-known is, for some, the very barrier to love.

However, Drs. Dahl, Stewart, Martell, and Kaplan walk the reader through a set of processes that create just the space in which intimacy in relationship is possible. The truly noteworthy feature of this book—and the basis of its utility—is the authors' theoretical understanding of ACT and RFT and their application to the creation of deep and meaningful relationships. The authors do not take the conventional path, which generally explores love and intimacy as parts of a plan for self-improvement leading to a felt positive state. Rather, they provide a behavior analytic conceptualization of love, linking this very human issue to a sound theoretical and scientific approach and a thorough understanding of human language and cognition. Do not be scared away by this distinctive part of the book. The behavior analytic approach forms the backbone of a technology that will guide him or her in the use of the intervention while promoting maximum flexibility in the therapy room.

In part 1, the authors introduce functional contextualism, basics in behavior analysis, the origins of love, and the problem of language as it relates to human relationship. Each concept is presented in a digestible fashion and linked to the exploration of love and intimacy in human connection. The reader will find this part of the book particularly useful in developing an intervention that's tailored to the personal histories, current context, and individual behavioral complexity of the couple presently in the therapy room.

Part 2 explores the moment of truth in intimate and healthy relationships. Relationships—as we know through experience but aren't necessarily taught—are not simply romantic in nature, or the stuff of fairy tales. They are about letting go of ideals and right and wrong; they are about occasionally suffering through lowered expectations and demands; they are about forgiveness, and self-compassion and -examination—and, yes, they are also about kindness, laughter, happiness, shared experience, and enhanced connection.

The authors of this book both capture this reality and, using ACT and RFT, provide readers with a way to instigate engaged and healthy relationships. The authors' focus in describing ACT and RFT as they apply to healthy human connection is on fostering personal flexibility in the service of committing to and honoring deeply held values—the true earth of long-lasting and deep relationships. The reader is invited to explore the processes of ACT that generate openness to experience, including mindfulness and acceptance, self-as-experiencer, and self-compassion. Each of these processes is designed to disentangle the client from the fear, dread, and secret-keeping that *seem* to prevent intimacy in relationships, freeing him or her to actively engage in behaviors centered on being loving.

The significance of this approach to intimacy is that it liberates the individual to act on building a way for personal "knownness" that can be shared with another as a matter of choice, rather than of feeling. This is not to say that feelings are not important; they surely are, as the authors of this book will also tell you. The difficulty arises when feelings become the arbiter of our life direction; they can, if followed blindly, leave us in fear and alone. Values-based choice is the antidote to this.

In *ACT and RFT in Relationships*, Drs. Dahl, Stewart, Martell, and Kaplan have lit a candle for your arrival; read the book and apply its knowledge. Helping clients to fully engage their values in efforts to define and grow intimate and healthy relationships, as these authors have done, is wonderful. Again, if there is anything better than to be loved, it is to *be* loving— and to do so as a chosen and fully lived value.

—Robyn D. Walser, PhD
Assistant Clinical Professor,
University of California, Berkeley
Associate Director, National Center for PTSD,
Dissemination and Training Division

Acknowledgments

To Dan, with appreciation for your persistency, patience, and passion in helping me open up a closed door and, in so doing, boost my exposure to and exploration and experience of the pain and the ecstasy of an intimate relationship.

—J.D.

To all those lovely people with whom I've shared some lovely moments.

—I.S.

Of the four authors of this book, I came to the project with the least knowledge of ACT and RFT. I am thankful, therefore, to have worked with such a brilliant team of fellow authors. I wish first to thank JoAnne Dahl for inviting me to join the project as an author. Though when we met we lived on different continents, we quickly learned that we each share the experience of childhoods growing up in the Green Mountains of Vermont. Working with Ian Stewart has given me the privilege of a practically private tutorial in RFT and the experience has been enlightening and fun, so I express my gratitude to Ian. Jonathan Kaplan came to the project at a time when we needed new energy, and he added just that. I've enjoyed working with this great team immensely!

My background is in behavioral treatments for individuals and couples. Andrew Christensen, PhD, and the late Neil S. Jacobson, PhD, invited me to be a research therapist on their multi-site couples therapy research program in the late 1990s, and that work changed my career and my life. I am particularly thankful to Andy for continuing to invite me to write with him on Integrative Behavioral Couples Therapy.

Finally I need to acknowledge my partner, Mark Williams, for his gentle and generous spirit and his ongoing support through the years.

— C.M.

I would like to thank my wife, Doris, and two sons, Eli and Reed, for helping me learn about love in a myriad of ways. They give me many opportunities to express love as a value and a behavior, while being able to experience it as a feeling as well (most of the time, anyway). A coterie of special people has guided me in learning how to love, including my parents, sister, and teachers: Tara Brach, Sharon Salzberg, and Laura O'Loughlin. Thank you very much for your tutelage and support. In addition, I'd like to thank my co-authors and intern Susanna Johansson for their unwavering support and judicious commentary. Writing this book together has been a real pleasure! Finally, I'd like to express my appreciation and gratitude for all of my past, present, and future patients. You all have shared your lives with me, in ways that are both touching and humbling. The gift of connection, aliveness, and presence in our meetings has been nourishing beyond measure. I feel grateful for the opportunity to bear witness to the pain you have experienced and to participate in your growth and recovery. Your efforts to live more mindfully and meaningfully are an inspiration.

—J.K.

CHAPTER 1

Introduction to Romantic Love

- ✦ Introduction
- ✦ Psychological Perspectives
- ✦ Problems with the Conventional View
- ✦ An Alternative Perspective
- ✦ Conclusion

Introduction

Romantic love is a meaningful experience for countless human beings. It can bring great joy, but it can also bring immense pain and suffering. Given the importance of love for so many people, it behooves us to understand it to the greatest extent possible in both its positive and its negative aspects.

The conventional view of romantic love is as an emotional experience. This view has become prevalent throughout the world and is especially well established in modern Western society. In many cultures, love in this sense, rather than duty or social standing, has become the predominant reason for people to establish long-term, committed relationships.

To date, psychological research as well has focused typically on the emotional aspects of love, which are sometimes conflated with cognitions and behaviors. Given that the field of psychology has been dominated by a focus on love as an emotion, we propose a different perspective. From the vantage point of modern behavioral analysis, and more specifically relational frame theory (RFT) and acceptance and commitment therapy (ACT), we suggest that to consider love *as valued action* offers a novel perspective, one that can lead to vibrant and fulfilling relationships. Before we introduce our perspective on love, however, let us discuss some of mainstream psychology's key ideas about love.

Psychological Perspectives

Across the ages, the subject of romantic love has been pondered and treated by philosophers, poets, songwriters, novelists, artists, and spiritual figures. In modern times, romantic love is celebrated in literature, music, visual art, and film, and it provides fodder for most daytime dramas and talk shows. However, it has only recently come under scrutiny within contemporary psychology.

In 1975, Elaine Hatfield, an early researcher on love, achieved notoriety when her federally funded study on the role of equity in romantic relationships was awarded the satirical "Golden Fleece Award," created by US Senator William Proxmire of Wisconsin to denote a waste of taxpayers' money. Proxmire publicly lambasted Hatfield's work, arguing that it was not appropriate to study love scientifically, and many people supported his view, on romantic, religious, and financial grounds (Hatfield, 2006). Yet, despite its inauspicious reception by some critics, research on love has continued and grown.

Love as an Emotion

Hatfield and Walster (1978) described two types of romantic love: *passionate love*, an intense emotional state characterized by longing, idealization, sexual attraction, and a desire to unite completely with another person; and *companionate love*, which reflects a similar kind of tenderness and affection, but is less sexualized. For many people, early in a relationship, the feeling of passionate love is high, but over time it declines (Acker & Davis, 1992). Conversely, companionate love gradually increases as partners spend more time together. While this general pattern is not true for all couples (Acevedo & Aron, 2009; Hatfield, Traupmann, & Sprecher, 1984; O'Leary, Acevedo, Aron, Huddy, & Mashek, 2012), the distinction between these two kinds of love has persisted in the literature.

Berscheid (2006) provided an analysis of love in a broader sense that is nonetheless relevant to an analysis of romantic love. Berscheid refers to *attachment love* and *compassionate love*. Attachment love is related to the bond that develops between

3

infants and caregivers (typically parents) and is thus not characteristic of romantic love. In feeling, it is more associated with maternal or paternal love. In contrast, compassionate love, with its concern for another's suffering and well-being, might emerge in romantic relationships. It is considered a selfless kind of emotion, in which one takes another's needs, wants, and pains to heart. It involves clearly seeing and valuing another with openness and receptivity (Underwood, 2008).

Sternberg's triangular theory of love (1986) provides another psychological perspective, incorporating emotions as well as cognitions. In this model, love is considered to involve three components: (1) *intimacy*, (2) *passion*, and (3) *decision/commitment*. Intimacy refers to the feelings of closeness and affection experienced in a relationship. Passion involves intense sexual attraction. Decision/commitment pertains to short-term and long-term decisions to stay with a particular partner. Sternberg suggests that different kinds of love emerge based on the interaction of these three factors. For example, infatuation comes of passion with little or no intimacy or commitment, and "empty love" emerges when there is commitment without any intimacy or passion. Tests of Sternberg's theory have involved the development of an appropriate survey instrument (e.g., Sternberg, 1997; Cassepp-Borges & Pasquali, 2012) and investigations of how well it describes long-term relationships (e.g., Acker & Davis, 1992).

Love in the Brain and Body

Interestingly, much of the research on love has focused on neurological phenomena. Neuroimaging of people experiencing passionate love,[1] for example, has shown activation in subcortical areas associated with emotions, rewards, and motivation, as well as cortical areas related to memory, attention, social cognition, and other higher-order brain functions (Aron et al., 2005; S. Cacioppo, Bianchi-Demicheli, Hatfield, & Rapson, 2012; Fisher, Aron, & Brown, 2006; Schneiderman, Zagoory-Sharon, Leckman, & Feldman, 2012). As anyone experiencing intense love can attest, the high level of subcortical activity in dopaminergic-related areas is similar to drug-induced euphoria (Acevedo, Aron, Fisher, & Brown, 2012). When in love, people feel "high" and "on top of the world." Research has even suggested that being in love can attenuate the cravings associated with withdrawal from addictive substances (Xu et al., 2012). Activation in these reward-related areas of the brain, as well as areas indicative of attachment and pair-bonding, can continue even over long-term relationships. Researchers have also found that the breakup of a romantic relationship can cause activity in brain regions associated with physical pain, thus giving credence to the popular maxim that love hurts (Kross, Berman, Mischel, Smith, & Wager, 2011). Taken together, these neurological studies of passionate love reveal that it activates brain areas associated with feelings, senses, and cognitions (Ortigue, Bianchi-Demicheli, Patel, Frum, & Lewis, 2010). As such, it provides some evidence for Lao-tzu's observation "Love

---

1 Though beyond the scope of this book, some studies have also examined the association between love and meditation. Specifically, researchers have examined the neurological correlates of engaging in metta meditation. Commonly translated as loving-kindness or friendliness, metta might most be associated with universal love, or agape. Results show that metta and compassion-based meditations do have particular profiles of neurological activity (e.g., Lee et al., 2012; Lutz, Brefczynski-Lewis, Johnstone, & Davidson, 2008).

is of all passions the strongest, for it attacks simultaneously the head, the heart, and the senses" (Lao-tzu, n.d.)

Most studies of the physical effects of love have examined people in long-term relationships. For example, one often-quoted statistic is that being in a good marriage promotes longevity: compared to unmarried people of the same gender, married men live about seven years longer, and married women live about three years longer (Parker-Pope, 2010). Conversely, the death of a spouse is considered one of the most stressful life experiences (Holmes & Rahe, 1967). Though these findings are intriguing, the degree to which they relate to love is unclear. For example, increased longevity might be related to partners taking care of each other and better caring for themselves.

Styles of Love

Lee (1977) proposed that people have particular ways of experiencing love, reflective of their social group membership. These styles include *eros* (romantic ideal), *judus* (game-playing), *storge* (slow-developing affection and friendship), *mania* (great emotional intensity), *agape* (altruistic), and *pragma* (rational consideration of which person constitutes an appropriate match). Categorically, these styles are representative of behavior, as well as emotions and love-related cognitions, and thus are perhaps more appropriately considered "ideologies" (Watts & Stenner, 2005). Interestingly, this concept of "love styles" has been examined from the point of view of attachment theory. Attachment style may be indicative of the kind of love that one will develop and experience later in life (e.g., Sprecher & Fehr, 2011).

Researchers also have made a distinction between love and sexual behavior. Various studies have revealed that, as anyone who has been in a relationship can attest, love and sex are related, but neither guarantees the presence of the other (Beck, Bozman, & Qualtrough, 1991; Regan, 2000). Gonzaga, Turner, Keltner, Campos, and Altemus (2006) argue that romantic love and sexual desire can be distinguished based on function (i.e., commitment versus reproduction) and on the emotional states and nonverbal displays involved.

In a recent study examining the ways in which men and women express love in marriage (Schoenfeld, Bredow, & Huston, 2012), some of the conventional stereotypes were supported (e.g., men are more likely to associate love and sex), but other findings suggest that love is more nuanced. For example, men were just as likely as women to express love through tenderness and affection. In addition, the study found that husbands in love are more likely to do housework and involve their partners in shared leisure activities.

Love as an Evolutionary Force

Love has also been viewed from an evolutionary perspective. Generally speaking, those adopting this point of view consider love to have adaptive functions that secure reproduction and survival (e.g., Buss, 2006). For example, passionate love allows for mating and a mutual investment in child-raising. Furthermore, parental love supplements romantic love in achieving these purposes, because love directed toward infants ensures their survival at a time when they are profoundly dependent. In these respects, love and the concomitant development of a long-term commitment between partners, referred to by evolutionary psychologists as "pair-bonding," have been evolutionarily adaptive. Indeed, evidence supporting this contention is that we are not the only species to have evolved pair-bonding and long-term commitment. However, when combined with the uniquely human phenomenon of symbolic language (whose effect we examine in later chapters), these evolved tendencies enable the experience of romance, which is indeed particular to our species.

Love as a Word

Some of the early research on love investigated the ascribed meanings that people attach to the word itself (e.g., Fehr, 1988). Perhaps not surprisingly, people have many different definitions of love. A factor analysis of the plethora of associations revealed that "love" is most commonly related with intimacy, commitment, and passion (Aron & Westbay, 1996). Thus when people talk about love, they mean many different things.

People often make a distinction between "loving" someone and "being in love" with someone (Meyers & Berscheid, 1997). The first is more reflective of companionate or compassionate love, while the second is more indicative of intense romantic feelings. Interestingly, these words and associations implicitly can serve as criteria for relationships. For example, when breaking up with someone, people often say, "I love you, but I'm not *in love* with you." Presumably, they are referring to the absence of passion, which has thus become a necessary ingredient for a serious relationship. Further, people sometimes complain about not feeling loved by their partner. In these cases, love is something that one receives from another, not simply in the form of behaviors, but also as a feeling generated in the one being loved.

Taken together, people's associations with the word "love" are complicated and reflect the fact that the experience is difficult to express. As Julia opines in Shakespeare's *Two Gentlemen of Verona*, "Didst thou but know the inly touch of love, / Thou wouldst as soon go kindle fire with snow / As seek to quench the fire of love with words" (2.7.18–20). In subsequent chapters, we explore the ways in which people relate verbally to love.

Love in Different Cultures

Some have suggested that romantic love might be a particularly Western phenomenon, characteristic of modern, industrialized countries. However, evidence increasingly suggests that romantic love is experienced in cultures across the world (Hatfield & Rapson, 2006). Cross-cultural studies further have suggested that passionate love is not a unidimensional construct, but rather composed of several related factors, including commitment, security, passion, affection, stability, and the degree to which people are focused on themselves or their partner (Landis & O'Shea, 2000). Thus, while it seems that romantic love is universal, its meaning and expression differ across cultures.

Love as a Feeling

As we have shown, psychologists have offered many different perspectives on love. Most of these, however, revolve around love as a feeling, sometimes conflating it with cognitions and behaviors as well. Even the "father of behaviorism," John Watson, succumbed to this romantic view of love when writing to his mistress: "Every cell I have is yours, individually and collectively. My total reactions are positive and towards you. So likewise each and every heart reaction. I can't be any more yours than I am even if a surgical operation made us one" (Buckley, 1994, p. 28). As this quote and the psychological approaches we have been considering suggest, the notion of love as a feeling is a particularly pervasive one within psychology. But let us consider problems with this idea of love as a feeling.

Problems with the Conventional View

Mainstream psychological perspectives on romantic love both originate in and support popular cultural conceptions of love. The shared conception that chiefly concerns us in this book is that of love as a feeling or emotion. In our modern Western culture, people talk about feelings, motives, longing, and needs in romantic relationships. However, when love is seen as something felt—and particularly as a "feel good" emotion—it can be problematic.

All the "feel good" aspects of love are nice. However, people may be set up for disappointment and failure when too much emphasis is placed on pure emotion as a driving force in relationships. Too often, people see love from the perspective of its impact on themselves, how another person makes them feel and how their needs are met, rather than a focus on attention to the other, the loved one. Since the start of the Romantic era in the eighteenth century, people have increasingly elevated love as the primary reason that relationships are formed and lifetime commitments made. However, when people seek and live relationships according to what they have been told in "happily ever after" fairy tales, they may paradoxically find themselves unfulfilled and unhappy. This paradox, and an alternative way to approach loving relationships, is at the heart of this book.

Love, Marriage, and...Disappointment?

Nowadays, marriage is typically considered the consummation of a romantic relationship. For example, one indication of the perceived social importance of marriage is the dispute over allowing same-sex couples to marry; whether people approve or disapprove of gay marriage, their feelings on the subject tend to be strong.

Throughout most of human history, legal partnerships or marriages were social contracts. Such social contracts helped people improve their social standing, legitimized the resulting children, and maintained inheritance rights (Coontz, 2005). According to Coontz, nearly as soon as love-based marriages became the fashion in the late nineteenth century, the divorce rate escalated. Coontz points out the irony that "the strongest opponents of divorce in the nineteenth century were traditionalists who disliked the exaltation of married love. They feared that making married love the center of people's emotional lives would raise divorce rates, and they turned out to be right" (p. 180). The lifelong commitment typified by marriage (i.e., "until death do us part") created more pressure on couples, making it even more difficult for them to live "happily ever after."

We can assume that the same joys and disappointments of relationships and marriage are experienced by same-sex couples. The limited data for couples in committed same-sex relationships suggest that they are just as contented and fulfilled as married heterosexual couples (Kurdek, 2005). Data on divorce rates for same-sex couples do not exist, but we can assume, given that data on same-sex couples indicate that they are as satisfied and committed as heterosexual couples (e.g., Kurdek, 1998), that they share the potential to have the same types of problems and miseries. In the latter respect, there are limited data to suggest that same-sex couples may, in fact, resolve conflict better than heterosexual couples (Gottman et al., 2003). Nevertheless, we await more same-sex marriages throughout the world in order to say whether these relationships are less likely to fail.

Relying on Feelings May Destabilize Relationships

One of the greatest problems with relying on a feeling of "being in love" as a guide to the health or vitality of a romantic relationship is that feelings may change. For many people, it is quite easy to fall in love, and it may be just as easy to fall out of love—perhaps when another, more attractive person comes along. The unreliable nature of feelings is the very reason that for most of human history, love was considered a poor justification for marriage (Coontz, 2005). Even if people care deeply for their partner, this doesn't mean that they will always be in touch with positive feelings; they will often have aversive feelings, such as doubt, irritation, hurt, and anger. When aversive feelings predominate, it can feel like "falling out of love." One might take this as an indication that he or she should no longer be with a particular partner, even though loving feelings can be rekindled. This is not to say that people should stay in unhappy relationships, but rather that, perhaps, there should be a focus on something other than positive feelings in romantic relationships.

The Problem Is Not Love, but Love "Filling a Void"

Let us be clear that we see nothing wrong with love, and we are not anti-love or anti-passion. In fact, throughout this book we present ideas that we hope will increase people's satisfaction, fulfillment, and passion through valued action rather than their acquiescence to a loveless life. While many would agree that it can feel very good to be in love, it is also good to recognize that the endless search for pleasure and "feeling good" can lead, ultimately and ironically, to unhappiness, particularly when it comes to intimate relationships. People often speak of "needs" when they refer to loving relationships—whether with partners or friends—and there may also be a paradox in that seeking to have a need met as a primary motivator for action may actually result in less happiness overall. There is even research to suggest that pursuing happiness as a goal actually results in increased feelings of loneliness (Mauss, Tamir, Anderson, & Savino, 2011; Mauss et al., 2012).

Reiterating That Love as a Feeling State Is Problematic

While there is no clear definition of what it means to be "in love," it appears to mean, at some level, enjoying the feeling generated by being with another person. To some extent, one loves how one feels in regard to another, but the feeling is self-centered. In this instance, when love is primarily experienced as a feeling state unconnected with actions taken according to personal or shared values, relationships may be more tenuous.

13

Because feelings change over time, it may be relatively easy to "fall out of love," as it can be to "fall in love." On the other hand, if couples act in a loving way, based on what they value about the relationship or according to values they share with their partner, they may find it easier to negotiate difficult times and disappointments.

An Alternative Perspective

We aim to describe the processes involved in romantic love in a way that may provide a better understanding and a guide to what is important in love and how people might have a more fulfilling type of love relationship. The alternatives that we propose in this book come from the field of behavior analysis. Behavior analysis approaches human experience from a scientific perspective. It investigates factors that influence behavior through systematic study of the relationships between environmental conditions and the resultant behaviors (Sulzer-Azaroff & Mayer, 1991). We consider it important to conceptualize romantic relationships, just like other areas of life, in terms of behavior-environment interactions. This allows us to understand these interactions from a natural science point of view.

Behavior Analysis, RFT, and ACT

Over the past two decades in particular, a promising new behavior analytic conceptualization of human language and cognition has been gaining empirical support. This approach, called relational frame theory (RFT; Dymond & Roche, 2013; Hayes, Barnes-Holmes, & Roche, 2001), represents a significant advance from traditional behavior analytic models of these phenomena (e.g., Skinner, 1957), including with respect to such critically important phenomena as thinking and feeling. This understanding of human behavior has had an impact with regard to practical application as well as theory. Perhaps the foremost example of this is that a new model of psychotherapy—acceptance and commitment therapy (ACT; Hayes, Strosahl, & Wilson, 1999)—has been developed in accordance with the same basic insights provided by RFT. This model offers a particular perspective on psychological fulfillment that is as relevant in the area of romantic relationships as it is in other areas of psychological importance in life. Thus, our speculations about the functions of love are founded on a modern scientific understanding of human thought and emotion. By building on this foundation, we hope to provide a guide to robust and fulfilling romantic relationships that go beyond a reliance on feeling good.

For us, a definition of love as valued action makes more sense than love as a feeling state. We are behavioral psychologists, and as such we believe that behavior analytic science has much to offer in the examination of how love as valued action can lead to better relationships in all their diversity. (This is the premise from which we write, and we say much about values, action, and human experience in this and later chapters of the book.) From a behavior analytic or functional contextual perspective (explained in chapter 2), all actions are "events" that occur in a particular context. Thus, in order to understand loving behavior, we must evaluate it as an "action in context" (a kind of "event in context"). The context in question includes sociocultural factors, the individual's learning history, events that have shaped his or her current behaviors and emotional responses, and the present contexts that maintain the behavior.

Broader Reinforcers in Relationships

Feeling love, passion, and excitement about someone because that person provides reasons to feel good is a powerful source of reinforcement that is commonly seen as paramount in intimate relationships. Falling out of love often occurs when feelings of love have not been reinforced by a partner's reciprocation. At such times, it might seem common sense that the timing is right to either seek therapy—typically to change aspects of the partner—or leave the relationship. However, there are other important sources of reinforcement for relationship behavior besides reciprocation. For example, it can be reinforcing to behave in ways that are consistent with one's values. According to ACT, people have hierarchies of values. The value of intimacy with another person might be high on anyone's hierarchy. Embodiment of this value might involve physical intimacy, open and honest communication, pursuit of shared activities, and many other possibilities available in day-to-day interactions. Enhanced engagement in these valued actions—rather than searching for happiness or fulfillment directly—may increase the likelihood that people ultimately will be happy and fulfilled in their relationships.

Not a Prescription

This book is not meant to propose any particular way that people should form relationships. As we've noted, throughout history, there have been many sociological changes in the purpose of marriage, the importance of marriage, the expectations of gender in relationships, the acceptability of same-sex unions, and many other areas related to our topic. And, based on the many configurations of couples, families, polygamous partnerships, and so forth that have developed over time, we cannot suggest that any one type of bond is ideal in an enduring sense, as we know that societies can change. Our premise that behavioral analysis, and specifically ACT/RFT, can take us on a new exploration of relationships does not imply that we oppose feeling happy, intimate, safe, and passionate in relationships—without such reinforcers, people would very likely never bother with relationships in the first place. Being human inherently involves establishing relationships and families, regardless of the particular structure. Further, just because we think of love as an action devoid of feelings, we are not proposing that anyone stay in an exploitative or abusive relationship. Acting lovingly is not to be confused with acting the martyr. To the contrary, an exploration of love as a value will reveal when to leave an unhealthy relationship and how to make a healthy one more vital and satisfying.

The Structure of This Book

In the first part of this book (chapters 1–4), we focus on the theories underlying our consideration of love. In chapter 2, we provide the philosophy and basic science underlying a behavioral perspective on love. We examine too the possible origins of love, specifically the contingencies of reinforcement at work during preverbal stages of child development. In chapter 3, we explore how language transforms basic processes and allows the complexity and subtlety of human life and human relationships. Language (or verbal behavior) is explained by the modern behavior analytic approach of RFT, which forms the theoretical basis for this chapter. The understanding of language processes provided by RFT, in turn, informs acceptance and commitment therapy, which focuses on values-based action and is at the heart of our current formulation. By beginning with the basic science of behavior analysis, we set the stage for understanding relationships in the applied arena, which constitutes the second part of this book. In chapter 4, we provide an overview of ACT and its relevance to love, relationships, and sexuality. In chapter 5, we focus on the pernicious influence of language, especially how people reify aspects of themselves based on what they think and say. This same process has consequences for relationships: people relate to others through their views of them, rather than through the qualities they manifest in particular moments, and such prejudices can cause conflicts and decrease the likelihood that disagreements will be resolved constructively. In chapter 6, we describe the deleterious effects of psychological rigidity and experiential avoidance, which include significant barriers to establishing loving relationships with others, despite people's best intentions. In chapter 7, we discuss the consideration of love as a value. We examine how people can realize this value in relationships without an unhealthy emphasis on emotions. In chapter 8, we examine a second potentially healthful phenomenon—self-compassion. We ask, "What would it look like to be in a relationship in which you have loving concern for yourself as well as for your partner?" In chapter 9, we examine evidence-based couples therapies from the perspectives of RFT and ACT. Through a case example, we propose alternative processes of change underlying particular techniques and approaches. Finally, in chapter 10, we provide concluding thoughts and a succinct summary.

Conclusion

Our intention in this book is to unite empirically based theories of psychology with a very complex aspect of human behavior. Insofar as behavioral analysis and RFT accurately reflect universal processes of human functioning, they should account for even the thorniest of issues, including love and how to improve intimate relationships. Much of what we propose in this book is speculative; the book is not meant as a self-help book for couples. Yet, in the coming chapters, we will propose a reasonable analysis of what can make romance so difficult and how anyone can make love a more satisfying, meaningful, and vital activity.

CHAPTER 2

The Roots of
Our Approach

+ Introduction

+ The Philosophy: Functional Contextualism

+ The Basic Science: Behavior Analysis

+ The Origins of Intimacy, Love, and Sexuality

+ Summary

Introduction

Romantic love is a topic in which many people are interested (to say the least!), and thus a lot has been written on this subject. However, we take a particular (and relatively unconventional) approach to this topic, since we aim to provide a scientific, psychological description of the processes involved, based on modern empirical insights into human behavior. This will help us provide some novel perspectives on this subject matter that hopefully will be illuminating as well as of practical benefit.

In this chapter and the following one, we provide the philosophical and scientific underpinnings of our approach. In the current chapter, we first describe functional contextualism, the philosophical worldview that underlies and shapes the whole of our scientific psychological approach. We then lay out important features of the science itself: behavior analysis, an empirically driven approach to understanding human behavior. From the behavior analytic perspective, people's behavior is shaped by interactions with their environment, including, of course, other people. Behavior analytic science provides us with the conceptual tools to understand the way in which this shaping occurs. It allows us to consider the ontogenic basis of romantic love—in other words, the learning that takes place in the typical person's life that shapes his or her romantic or loving behavior.

In order to fully understand the phenomenon of romantic love, it is important to understand one aspect of human behavior that has more influence than any other: human language. In the next chapter, we describe a modern behavior analytic theory of human language, relational frame theory (RFT), which has radically extended the reach of traditional behavior analysis by allowing the effective consideration of complex human behavior. The RFT approach to language also has implications for the improvement of human functioning, and coheres in a model based in the concept of psychological flexibility. This model is represented primarily by acceptance and commitment therapy (ACT), the widely applicable approach to achieving psychological fulfillment that we discuss in detail in chapter 4.

Understanding both RFT and ACT is critical to understanding our approach to romantic love. However, in order to understand RFT and ACT, it is important to understand and appreciate the philosophy and basic science that underlie them in their turn. Let us start with the philosophy: functional contextualism.

The Philosophy: Functional Contextualism

Science operates on the basis of fundamental assumptions. These assumptions determine the type of answers given to questions concerning the nature of reality, truth, and science itself. For example, what is the best way to think about reality? What is the nature of truth, and thus what "counts" as scientific evidence for a proposition? Ultimately, is science about discovering lots of facts, or is it about achieving goals?

Stephen C. Pepper (1942) suggested that philosophical assumptions can be organized into a small number of different worldviews, and that a person's worldview will determine his or her answers to the sorts of questions above. This, in turn, shapes what kinds of questions they might ask about the subject matter in which they are interested and what kind of answers might be satisfactory. Thus, from this perspective, it is important to be clear about worldview and assumptions. Worldviews can be explained in terms of key properties, including, perhaps most importantly, (a) a root metaphor, which is basically a simplified idea of what the world is like, and (b) a truth criterion, which determines what counts as truth.

Within the field of science, the most prevalent worldview by far is that of *mechanism*. From a mechanistic perspective, the world is, metaphorically, a giant machine composed of parts and forces, and the job of the scientist is to identify the parts of the machine that are relevant to the phenomenon in which he or she is interested and figure out how they work together to give rise to it.

The prototypical example of mechanism in the world of psychology is cognitive psychology's conception of humans as computers that take information in through the senses, process it, and emit appropriate behavioral output. Exploring human psychology from this perspective has typically involved developing models of cognition and then using controlled experiments to test predictions made on the basis of these models.

The mechanistic worldview has been extraordinarily successful in many areas of science, particularly in the so-called hard sciences (e.g., physics and chemistry). This success over the course of the past few centuries is no doubt why it has been adopted by scientists in diverse fields of exploration (including the human or social sciences) and underscores its popularity as the idea of how science operates.

The metaphor of the machine leads to an analytic view of reality that has been highly productive in such domains as physics and chemistry, whose subject matter is readily deconstructed and analyzed in terms of constituent parts whose operation is relatively independent of their context. However, it has proven less useful in other realms, particularly those involving human behavior, in which it becomes reductionistic. In psychology, for example, though the cognitive metaphor of human as computer has allowed limited prediction of specific forms of behavior under relatively controlled circumstances (e.g., experiments), it has arguably failed to yield effective ways of understanding human activity in broader, more meaningful contexts.

The truth criterion of the mechanistic worldview is correspondence between the scientist's predictions or hypotheses and the way the world is in fact found to work through empirical testing. In other words, there must be a correspondence between theory and reality. In psychology, the adoption of this criterion means that a theory is acceptable if its specification of the operation of cognition allows prediction of human behavior. However, while truth defined in this way might be acceptable from an academic perspective, it does not require practical intervention with respect to human behavior and does not readily lead to the development of such interventions. For example, we might argue that cognitive psychology has led to the creation of a vast multitude of models of aspects of cognition, but relatively little in the way of practical interventions to actually change human behavior. This lack of practical applications for knowledge of psychology is a serious one.

The psychological approach adopted in this book is founded on an alternative worldview called *contextualism*. The root metaphor of contextualism is the "event in context," in which every phenomenon is an "event" that happens in a context that determines the nature of that event. From this perspective, we cannot ignore the context, since without it the event would not be the same. For example, a kiss might be a sign of affection, but it might also be an act of betrayal; knowing whether the context was a meeting between Romeo and Juliet or one between Judas and Jesus helps us determine the meaning of the event.

The truth criterion of contextualism is successful work toward the analytic goal, whatever it might be. One important function of this criterion is that it delimits the amount of contextual information that is needed. Though the ultimate context for any event is the whole universe, it is typically unnecessary to examine context on such a grand scale, because we need only enough information to achieve the goal. In *descriptive contextualism*, the goal is a harmonious understanding of events. In *functional contextualism*—the form of contextualism underlying our present approach—the goal is to predict and influence events.

In psychology, the "events" we are interested in are human actions. These actions always happen in a context that determines their nature. The contextualist worldview, which naturally takes situational determinants of behavior into account, lends itself to the study of complex human behaviors that happen in the context of other people, and involve thoughts and feelings that are the product of a complex and extended learning history. Functional contextualism is a variation of the contextualist worldview that seeks practical behavioral change. From this perspective, it is not enough to acknowledge the complexity of the human situation; we must achieve desired change. Thus, functional contextualism lends itself to the complexity of the human situation while also facilitating useful action in respect of that situation.

The Basic Science:
Behavior Analysis

Having introduced functional contextualism as the worldview underlying our approach, we next introduce behavior analysis, the psychological science based on this worldview that provides the theoretical and empirical roots of our approach.

Behavior Analysis as Functional Contextualism

Behavior analysis has been argued to possess both mechanistic and contextualistic aspects. However, it has been most convincingly interpreted as an example of a contextualist approach to psychology and as a prime example, in particular, of functional contextualism (Hayes, Hayes, & Reese, 1988).

Consideration of key features of behavior analytic science supports this view. For example, the explicitly stated goal of behavior analysis is prediction and influence over behavior (Hayes et al., 1988), which obviously coheres with the truth criterion of functional contextualism. A consequence of this goal is behavior analysis's insistence on the specification of environmental variables that allow both prediction of and influence over behavior.

Another key feature of behavior analysis that is functional contextualist in character is its core analytic unit, the operant. From a behavior analytic perspective, organisms respond to, or "operate," on their environment in particular ways, and their environment in turn provides consequences contingent on those responses that affect the likelihood that they will reoccur. This idea exemplifies the "action in context," the root metaphor of functional contextualism.

The Operant

Let us consider the operant more closely, since this is a key element of the behavior analytic conceptualization of human behavior and one that lies at the heart of key aspects of the overarching approach. The operant is also referred to as the

27

three-term or *ABC* contingency, where A stands for the antecedent (i.e., what precedes a particular response), B stands for behavior (i.e., the response itself), and C stands for consequence (i.e., the effect of the response).

At the core of this concept is the behavior itself—what the person does—and this can include simple actions, such as clicking one's fingers or smiling, as well as more complex actions, such as organizing a party or writing a book. From a behavior analytic perspective, actions such as these happen in context. This context includes any consequences of actions that make them either more or less likely to reoccur in the future, and it also includes any antecedents that signal what the consequences of a possible behavior are likely to be. Within behavior analysis, all three factors (antecedent, behavior, and consequence) function as the operant, not just the behavior itself.

Consequences

Consequences that make an action more likely to reoccur are referred to as *reinforcers*. Some consequential stimuli can be classified as *primary* or *biological* reinforcers; these include food, drink, warmth, sleep, and sex, which we as a species are evolutionarily disposed to find reinforcing because being motivated to work for these things is important for our survival and reproduction. In addition to primary consequential stimuli, there are *secondary* or *conditioned* reinforcers, which acquire their effect by being associated with primary ones. Learning through stimulus association is a simple but powerful mode of learning referred to as *respondent* or *associative* conditioning. An example in the case of reinforcers is that the attention, affection, and approval of certain people become conditioned reinforcers through association with primary reinforcers that these people can provide, such as food and warmth in the case of parents and sex in the case of potential sexual partners. Other conditioned reinforcers are money, educational achievement, and problem-solving success.

Consequences that make an action less likely to reoccur are referred to as *punishers*. Just as there are primary and secondary reinforcers, so too are there primary and secondary punishers. Primary punishers include pain and cold, because such conditions are potential threats to survival, while secondary punishers include stimuli associated with these or with the loss of reinforcers. For example, social disapproval may be associated with the loss of primary or secondary reinforcers, including affection or sex.

Consequences can involve either the receipt of a stimulus or the removal of a stimulus, and either of these types of consequence can be reinforcing or punishing. An increase in behavior due to the addition of a stimulus is known as *positive reinforcement*. For example, if you smiled at another person more often when the other person reliably smiled back, we would say that your smiling was positively reinforced. Further, the smiling of the other person is referred to as a *reinforcing* or *appetitive stimulus*. When an increase in behavior is due to the removal of a stimulus—for example, when an increase in cooperative behavior by little Jimmy reliably stops or prevents his mother from frowning at him—this is referred to as *negative reinforcement*. With regard to the latter, a behavior that increases because it actively removes a stimulus (e.g., Jimmy's mother is frowning at him; Jimmy starts cooperating, and this stops her from frowning) is known as *escape*, whereas a behavior that increases in order to prevent something from happening (e.g., Jimmy acts cooperatively in order that his mother will not begin frowning) is known as *avoidance*. Punishment involves either the addition of something aversive or unpleasant (e.g., Jimmy is yelled at by his mother) or the removal of something appetitive or pleasant (e.g., Jimmy is temporarily barred from playing with toys).

One other set of concepts important with respect to the science of consequences is the *establishing operation* (EO) or *motivational operation* (MO; see, e.g., Michael, 1982). These terms refer to procedures or processes that increase or decrease the effectiveness of particular consequences as reinforcers or punishers. For example, food or sex become even more reinforcing after you have been deprived of them, yet they can become aversive if you are already satiated.

Antecedents

The relationship between actions and their consequences is one type of important behavior-environment relationship. Another is the influence of the antecedent, or *discriminative stimulus*. This element signals what the consequences of a possible behavior are likely to be. For example, if you are in conversation with your friend Theresa and she is acting in a cheerful manner (the antecedent—A), then your smiling at her (the behavior—B) is likely to be met with a smile and continued conversation (the consequence—C), whereas if she is acting in a downcast or angry manner (A), then smiling at her (B) may produce an angry reaction (C). With regard to both cases, we can say that the manner in which your friend Theresa is acting is functioning as an antecedent, or discriminative stimulus, for particular consequences contingent on your particular behavior.

The Operant as Class Concept

You should note that operant-relevant concepts, such as reinforcement, punishment, and discrimination, are functional class concepts—they are defined based on observed patterns of behavior-environment relations. One of the results of this is that stimuli or responses are *not* classified on the basis of presumed psychological effect or the topography of the events involved.

For example, a smile might be presumed to act as a reinforcer, and a frown as a punisher, but as we have just shown, these topographies need not function so in either case. As another example, in a context in which you "open up" to your partner about something you consider to be a serious and problematic issue, you might take a smile to mean that he or she doesn't take your problem seriously, whereas you might take a frown or earnest expression to mean the opposite. These interpretations of your partner's behavior, which are determined by your learning history with smiles and frowns, will influence your behavior. In the first case (your partner smiles), you may be less likely to confide in your partner in the future, whereas in the second (your partner frowns) you may be *more* likely to do so; hence a smile in this example is punishing, whereas a frown is reinforcing. The key point is that the psychological function of stimuli (for example, whether they function as reinforcers or punishers) always depends on their relationship with other aspects of the context.

The point just made is simple enough. However, there are also slightly more abstract issues to consider. One such issue is that operant concepts, such as reinforcement, are based on patterns of events in behavior-environment relations rather than on singular events.

Consider the example of John, who starts to smile more at Jane when she consistently returns his smile. Someone who sees John smile at Jane and sees Jane smile back *could not* classify this as an example of reinforcement, because no increase in John's behavior of smiling at Jane has been observed—only a single smile on John's part and Jane's reaction. Only on the basis of observing an increase in John's rate of smiling based on Jane's returned smile could the observer note that reinforcement had occurred. More specifically, only on the basis of (a) measuring the rate at which John smiled at Jane before she started to smile back and (b) demonstrating an increase in that rate once she began to reciprocate his smile would someone be able to refer to this as an example of reinforcement. Thus, reinforcement is a pattern of behavior-environment relations over time, not simply a single series of events (i.e., John smiling and Jane smiling back). For the same reason, the behavioral and environmental events involved in reinforcement are not single events but classes of events. For instance, the response in the above example is not a single action (e.g., one particular instance of John's smiling) but a class of actions (i.e., John's smiling responses), while the consequence is not one particular instance of Jane returning John's smile, but the class of stimulus events "Jane smiling back at John." The same reasoning also applies to the antecedent for John's response, which in this case would be seeing Jane look in his direction. Again, it would not be one instance of this stimulus event but the class of events "Jane looking in John's direction" that would be relevant.

The fact that the events involved in the operant are classes of events rather than single events means that behavior can change and evolve in various ways, and these are also important aspects of learning. The fact that the response is a class event allows *response induction*, whereby the person starts to show not just the originally reinforced response, but also other responses that are physically similar to the first. For example, when a child learns to speak, the child may receive reinforcement for producing a particular sound and may subsequently produce not only that same sound but variations on it as well. The opposite of response induction is *response differentiation*, whereby responding becomes more precise. For example, someone who regularly practices tennis gradually becomes better at hitting the ball so that it lands inside the lines on the other side of the court.

There are also the phenomena of *generalization* and *discrimination*, which come about based on the fact that the antecedent, or discriminative stimulus, is a class event. For example, after little Juliana has learned to desist from whatever she is doing when her mother or father tells her, "Stop," she might also desist when other adults tell her, "Stop," thus generalizing from her parents. In an example of the opposite of this process—discrimination—she might eventually learn to selectively obey certain adults including her mother and father and certain other authority figures (e.g., her teacher) but not others, including strangers.

The Origins of Intimacy, Love, and Sexuality

In this section, we explain how the key concepts of behavior analytic science that we have outlined might aid an understanding of early learning foundations of romantic love.

Early Childhood

From a behavior analytic perspective, the importance of love and intimacy in humans has its origins in the fact that, as is the case with many other animals, humans are helpless at birth and are therefore evolutionarily predisposed to seek biological sustenance from a primary caregiver, usually the mother. In behavior analytic terms, the caregiver is therefore the key source of a number of primary reinforcers, including food, warmth, and stimulation. From a behavioral perspective, the fact that the caregiver provides these reinforcers means that the caregiver has become a conditioned (secondary) reinforcer and, as a result, attaining proximity to the caregiver becomes an end in itself for the child.

It is likely that a predisposition on the part of the child toward establishing a bond with the caregiver is also an important legacy of the evolutionary process. The extent to which this bonding is hardwired versus learned through processes of reinforcement is an empirical question (see, e.g., Harlow & Zimmermann, 1958, for relevant empirical research). In any event, the infant quickly comes to discriminate the face of the caregiver from other faces and also to discriminate particular facial expressions of the caregiver, such as smiling, that are predictive of the provision of primary reinforcers (e.g., stimulation) and secondary reinforcers (e.g., attention).

Of course, it seems likely that there is also a predisposition on the part of the caregiver to establish a bond with the child. Both child and caregiver find interaction with the other reinforcing, and their interaction becomes more complex and differentiated over time. One feature of the interaction is imitation (a key form of operant behavior; see Baer, Petersen, & Sherman,

34

1967); the child may copy the smile on the face of the caregiver, for example. The example of smiling is a particularly important one, since smiling when another person smiles is a socially powerful form of imitation and one that, especially in the case of the child-caregiver interaction, can stimulate further bonding. This form of imitation is also a precursor for more advanced forms of imitation, including echoic behavior, in which the child echoes sounds produced by the caregiver.

Another feature of the child-caregiver interaction is the importance of eye contact (e.g., Farroni, Csibra, Simion, & Johnson, 2002). Eye contact is stimulating and thus reinforcing for both parties, and playing eye-contact games develops into joint attention games, in which one party draws the attention of the other to an interesting object by looking from the object to the eyes of the other person and back again.

Imitation of smiling, eye contact, and joint attention are important elements of the child-caregiver interaction, and they lead to a strong bond. These are learned mutually reinforcing patterns of behavior. As such, they not only unite child and caregiver; they also provide an important training context for the child that establishes many of the features that will characterize his or her sexual intimacy in adulthood.

Middle Childhood

A child's relationship with his or her caregiver provides the child a first and no doubt fundamentally physically and psychologically important example of an intimate affectionate relationship. The child-caregiver relationship will continue to be of importance to the child as he or she develops. In addition to the experience of intimacy or affection, other basic psychological phenomena linked with this relationship are relevant to patterns of love and romantic behavior later on in life. In particular, children learn about sex and gender roles during middle childhood.

Children typically learn relatively early to discriminate between male and female characteristics and between masculine and feminine types of behavior, and they often acquire aspects of sexual identity by imitating the behavior of a caregiver of the same sex (e.g., Bandura, 1977). In addition, most caregivers will at least implicitly reinforce this and other gender-typical behavior while discouraging gender-atypical behavior, and some will train these behaviors explicitly (e.g., Block, 1979). Aspects of the way in which caregivers interact with each other may also provide a template for children with respect to their interactions with other people—in particular, members of the opposite sex. For example, if the father is generally dominant, while the mother is generally submissive, then this may affect the child's learning of gender roles (i.e., through imitation) and thus his or her interaction with peers of both sexes in childhood and later on. The child may learn to generalize from these exemplars to males and females more generally, and the extent to which the child does so may determine the extent to which he or she holds stereotypical attitudes with respect to gender roles.

Caregivers' attitudes toward sex and their public displays of loving or sexual behavior with each other may also affect their children's learning with respect to these. For example, the extent to which caregivers reflect anxiety and embarrassment versus openness and ease concerning sex may differentially affect their children's ease of dealing with sexual issues themselves.

Late Childhood and Early Puberty

The child-caregiver bond remains relatively strong throughout childhood, though it becomes less salient as the child becomes less dependent on the provision of reinforcers by the caregiver. For example, the relationship weakens as the child acquires friends and the interactive stimulation provided by the parent consequently becomes relatively less important. The relationship's significance declines further when the child starts to develop into a sexual being, around the start of puberty. The child's peer group, including members of the opposite sex, will often become a strong focus of attention as hormonal and other physical changes establish sexual contact as an increasingly important source of reinforcement.

In early puberty, many children begin to act so as to gain attention and affection from peers—for example, by imitating members of their peer group or acting in extreme and attention-grabbing ways. The attention of caregivers becomes somewhat punishing for these children, since it tends to be predictive of restriction and opposition to their new behavioral repertoires, especially if caregivers attempt to control or influence their behavior.

The child-caregiver interaction provides an important template for adult sexual relationships, and as the child becomes a sexual being, he or she may duplicate some of the same intimate interactions that provided him or her with such powerful reinforcement as an infant with peers to whom he or she is sexually attracted. What the child has previously learned from caregivers with respect to gender roles, as well as with respect to attitudes toward sex and sexual behavior, will also influence interactions with peers. Imagine, for example, that a child had been raised in a family in which the caregivers did not display affection for each other while in the presence of their children. The absence of any models for intimate behavior at home might cause the child to be unsure and awkward in expressing affection toward others and hence he or she might seek examples elsewhere (e.g., film or TV).

Basic behavioral processes are important in shaping learning with respect to loving and sexual behavior. The kinds of basic processes that we have identified (reinforcement, punishment, discrimination, generalization, etc.) are especially influential for young children who are still developing language ability. However, verbal ability dramatically influences human learning, and, thus, as language becomes well established, any analysis of human learning must take this phenomenon into account. Hence, in order to fully explain human learning with respect to love and sexuality, it is necessary for us to first discuss verbal processes and the psychological phenomena to which they give rise. This is the aim of the next two chapters.

Summary

In this chapter, we introduced the philosophy and basic science underlying our approach to love and sexuality. The philosophy is a form of contextualism that focuses on the "action in context" and a form of pragmatism that orients the science that it supports toward changing rather than simply predicting behavior. We examined such core concepts of the basic science as reinforcement, punishment, discrimination, and generalization. These concepts are important with respect to understanding the development of human love and sexuality from an early age.

This is partly because they allow us to consider the way in which these processes can influence development directly. However, it is also important because understanding these processes is critical in comprehending the nature and origins of relational framing, which underlies sophisticated human behavior, including romantic love and sexuality. In the next chapter, building on the foundations established here, we focus on relational framing.

Chapter 3

Relational Frame Theory

Introduction

In the previous chapter, we introduced the basics of the behavior analytic approach to psychology. We then used these concepts to guide an understanding of relationships—the psychological roots of love and romance—in early human learning. However, this was only a foundation for a more complete account. Once children learn language, their responding becomes increasingly complex, and nonverbal modes of learning become relatively less important for understanding their behavior. However, it is these later stages, especially adolescence and adulthood, that we particularly need to understand in all their complexity if we are to understand and appreciate human love and sexuality.

In order to provide a more complete behavioral account of language and complex human behavior including romantic love, we turn to relational frame theory (RFT; Hayes et al., 2001), which is the application of behavior analytic science to language and cognition. According to RFT, humans learn to respond in accordance with a variety of abstract relational patterns called relational frames, and these repertoires facilitate human language and enable the full range and subtlety of complex human behavior, including romance and love. This account provides us with a basic theoretical conceptualization of romantic behavior. It also informs the general approach to psychological health represented by acceptance and commitment therapy, which we explicate in the next chapter and use to suggest how people might get the most out of their romantic relationships. Hence, RFT is at the center of our approach; thus, this chapter constitutes an important foundation for our message.

At the core of the RFT approach is the understanding that from an early age, humans learn to rapidly and profoundly change the psychological functions of their environment. They begin to experience and interact with the world in ways that no other species does.

The Nature and Origins of Relational Framing

Ultimately, any animal's survival is based on its ability to interact accurately and adaptively with its environment. Accordingly, it is important for animals to make distinctions between prey and predator, mate and competitor, offspring and stranger, and so on.

Many species learn to relate things based on physical properties. For example, they can learn to discern that something is physically the same as or different from something else or that something is physically bigger or smaller than they are (e.g., Giurfa, Zhang, Jenett, Menzel, & Srinivasan, 2011). This is a type of relational responding called *non-arbitrary* relational responding. The relations are "non-arbitrary" in the sense that they are not subject to change based on human whim or convention. Humans, however, can also learn what is referred to as *arbitrarily applicable* relational responding, in which they relate objects based on contextual cues that specify the appropriate relation such that it can be applied no matter what the actual physical relations are. Such contextual cues can be "arbitrary" in the sense that they need not be based on an experienced interaction with the object and/or can "override" actual experience.

For example, if you tell a sufficiently verbal child that an imaginary animal called a "cug" is smaller than another imaginary animal called a "vek" and then ask, "Which is bigger, the cug or the vek?" the child will be able to give you the correct answer, even though he or she hasn't been told it and has obviously not come in contact with the animals in question. Physical relations don't matter in this case, because the child has learned to respond appropriately to the cues "smaller" and "bigger." Or, take another example, involving human relationships. Suppose that you tell the same child about two completely fictional characters, Muzzy and Hairgog, in the context of a story, and you say that Muzzy is meaner than Hairgog. Again, if you ask a question like, "Who is nicer, Muzzy or Hairgog?" the child will be able to answer correctly, even though he or she hasn't been told the answer and has obviously never met the individuals in question. Actual experience with these characters doesn't matter in this case, because the child has learned to respond appropriately to the cues "nicer" and "meaner."

The Variety of Frames

Arbitrarily applicable relational responding is also referred to as *relational framing*. It is based on the idea that, just as a picture frame can hold any picture no matter the picture's particular content, a relational frame can be applied to any stimulus no matter its physical properties. Furthermore, just as picture frames come in different shapes and sizes, there are multiple varieties of relational frame. The example just provided is an example of comparative relational framing, but people learn many other relational frames, including coordination (or sameness; e.g., in the simple sum "1 + 1 = 2," the "=" sign is a contextual cue for sameness), distinction (e.g., a tiger is different from a lion), opposition (e.g., day is opposite to night), hierarchical (e.g., an apple is a type of fruit), analogical (e.g., love is a battlefield), and deictic (perspective-taking; e.g., I am here and you are there). Furthermore, RFT researchers have provided a considerable quantity of empirical evidence for a variety of relational frames (e.g., Y. Barnes-Holmes, Barnes-Holmes, Smeets, Strand, & Friman, 2004; Y. Barnes-Holmes,

Barnes-Holmes, & Smeets, 2004; Berens & Hayes, 2007; Carpentier, Smeets, & Barnes-Holmes, 2003; McHugh, Barnes-Holmes, Barnes-Holmes, & Stewart, 2006; Roche & Barnes, 1997; Rosales, Rehfeldt, & Lovett, 2011; Steele & Hayes, 1991; Stewart, Barnes-Holmes, & Roche, 2004; see also Dymond, May, Munnelly, & Hoon, 2010; Rehfeldt & Barnes-Holmes, 2009).

The Origins of Framing

Relational frame theory sees arbitrarily applicable relational responding as an operant (see chapter 2), and it suggests that children learn this operant through exposure to multiple natural language interactions with caregivers and other verbal members of their community. The very earliest relational pattern that children learn is the bidirectional relation between words and objects. In this case, caregivers often reinforce a child's orienting to an object when its name is spoken (Name A → Object B; e.g., the caregiver says, "apple" → the child looks to or points at an apple) and reinforce speaking the name when the object is shown (Object B → Name A; e.g., the caregiver shows the child an apple, perhaps with the prompt "What's this?" → the child says, "apple"). This kind of interaction, in which both directions of the relational pattern are explicitly taught, happens countless times with numerous different objects (including social objects, of course, such as "Mommy" and "Daddy") until eventually the child has acquired the operant of bidirectional name-object relations. At that point, training in one direction (e.g., being told, "This [novel object A] is a [novel name B]") allows derivation in the other direction (i.e., after being asked where the [novel name B] is, the child readily points to novel object A). This bidirectional name-object pattern is particularly important, as it constitutes the key linguistic phenomenon of reference and also provides the foundation for the relational frame of coordination, which appears to be one of the most common and important frames in human language. After learning to respond to a relation of sameness between two stimuli (name and object), children subsequently learn, through continued exposure to natural language as well as through formal education, to combine two member relations into novel relations (e.g., if A is B and B is C, then A is C and C is A) and also to respond to noncoordinate relational frames such as those listed above.

Properties of Relational Framing

Hence, through exposure to the socio-verbal environment, children gradually acquire a variety of relational frames. From an RFT perspective, all frames have three characteristics. The first is *mutual entailment*, whereby a relation in one direction entails a relation in the other. For example, if you tell John, "Sally is more outgoing than Mary," then he can derive the relation "Mary is less outgoing than Sally." The second characteristic is *combinatorial entailment*, whereby two relations combine to entail additional relations. For example, if you tell John, "Sally is more outgoing than Mary" and also "Mary is more outgoing than Josephine," then he can derive both that Sally is more outgoing than Josephine and that Josephine is less outgoing than Sally. The third characteristic is *transformation of stimulus functions* via relational frames. For example, imagine that John is attracted to extroverted women and has to choose which of these three women (Sally, Mary, or Josephine) he'd prefer to go out with on a date. Even though he has never met any of them, and without knowing any more than the above facts, he might be most likely to choose Sally. The functions of the arbitrary stimuli "Sally," "Mary," and "Josephine" have been transformed (through relational frames) for our protagonist in such a way that he is drawn toward one of the women thus named.

The Transformative Effect of Relational Framing

The transformation of stimulus functions is a particularly important effect, as it describes the way in which relational framing can affect people's behavior by changing the functions of their environment. RFT defines a verbal stimulus as one whose functions have been transformed via relational frames, and thus this is the RFT explanation of the effect of language. From this perspective, as soon as children learn to relationally frame, stimuli in their environment start to become verbal and to serve new functions for them on that basis (just as the words "Sally" and "Josephine" did in the example above). This process changes both their environment and how they respond to it much more rapidly than other, more traditional behavioral processes.

Furthermore, the process of relationally framing objects and events is supported and advanced by continued interaction with the verbal community, and thus the networks of relations in accordance with which children respond continue to change and expand—hence these networks affect children to an increasing extent and in increasingly complex and subtle ways as they grow into adults.

Thus, from an early age, relational framing—the process underlying language—starts to change one's environment, and its influence tends to become more and more pervasive over time.

RFT and the Human Condition

Let us examine several ways in which relational framing can change a person's environment. In this section, we consider several important features of human psychology made possible by relational framing that are relevant to explaining complex human behavior, including the processes involved in acceptance and commitment therapy as well as human love and sexuality.

Bidirectional Stimulus Relations

Relational framing allows bidirectional, or mutually entailed, relations between stimuli. The most obvious and common example of this, of course, is the relation of reference between a word and an object. In this case, if an object is related to a word, then the word is also related to the object, and vice versa. The ability to relate stimuli in either direction importantly distinguishes human beings from other species, as we explain below.

Unidirectional vs. Bidirectional

For other species, conditioning is unidirectional. In the case of a dog, for instance, if an initially neutral stimulus (NS; e.g., the spoken word "biscuit") regularly precedes an unconditioned stimulus (UCS; e.g., a dog biscuit), then the NS will gain the psychological functions of the UCS and become a conditioned stimulus (CS). For example, on being presented with the CS (i.e., on hearing the word "biscuit"), the dog might salivate. However, this conditioning only works if the NS precedes the UCS. If instead of regularly saying "biscuit" before giving the dog a biscuit, you regularly give the dog the biscuit first, then say "biscuit," there is likely to be no conditioning. In other words, the word by itself will elicit no reaction. However, thanks to relational framing, for humans, conditioning is strongly bidirectional. For example, if you present a child with a cookie, and only tell the child that it is a "cookie" after he or she has received it, the child will still respond to the sound "cookie" later on, perhaps by remembering the look or taste of the cookie or by demonstrating interest. This is because the child frames the sound "cookie" and the actual cookie in a relation of sameness, and there is transformation of stimulus functions through this sameness relation such that the sound acquires the psychological functions of the object.

Bidirectionality: Positive and Negative

The bidirectionality inherent in relational framing can be hugely positive and beneficial. As we have explained, RFT sees relational framing as the process that characterizes language; and, since it also sees the latter as the basis of human cognition, then relational framing also becomes the basis of human cognition. From this perspective, then, it is the capacity to relationally frame that allows humans uniquely to remember and relive pleasant past events by discussing or thinking about them. Humans can analyze their past experiences and thus gain insight beyond that provided by contingency-shaping alone.

They can symbolize and think about aspects of their past and present environment in order to problem solve, as well as to plan for the future.

However, relational framing ability can also be a negative. Just as people can remember and imagine pleasant events, they can remember and imagine unpleasant ones; and just as they can plan for the future, they can spend their time worrying unnecessarily about it. Such experiences are an aversive but unavoidable aspect of being a verbal organism. However, the capacity for such experiences can also lead to *experiential avoidance*, in which people attempt to avoid unpleasant thoughts or emotions, an effort that can potentially interfere with their lives.

Consider someone who was abused as a child and who finds it extremely difficult to be intimate with a partner as an adult. The same person may also find it difficult to talk to a therapist about the abuse, despite knowing that the therapist might be able to help because the human ability to relationally frame means that the person's conditioning is bidirectional—talking about the abuse acquires the functions of the abuse itself. Talking about the abuse to a therapist would thus bring up aversive memories, including feelings of fear, shame, and self-loathing. In order to avoid this aversive experience, the person may avoid therapy. Avoiding therapy comes with a price, however, because difficulties being intimate with a partner constrain the person's ability to live a fully valued life.

Relational Coherence

The socio-verbal community not only teaches people to relationally frame, it also teaches coherence (i.e., sense-making) in relational framing. Coherence means that patterns of relational framing should cohere with or support rather than contradict each other—for example, "If my friend Gemma is nine, then she cannot also be ten." Relational coherence is highly advantageous, since it allows better prediction of and influence over others' behavior.

Generally, from an early age, coherence is reinforced and lack of coherence is punished. For example, a caregiver might frown and provide corrective feedback if a child uses the wrong name for an object or person, especially if the child does so repeatedly. Of course, there is an important context in which providing the wrong name or description for a person or thing might not be punished but instead be reinforced. In humor, deliberately using a wrong name, for example, might be reinforced by attention and shared amusement. However, humor works based on a shared understanding of a lack of coherence in a particular local context, which, in turn, requires an understanding of the coherent relations in the broader context, so ultimately even in humor, coherence is critical. Coherence also comes to be associated with successful problem solving in both the physical and social environments. Hence, for these reasons, relational coherence becomes a powerful conditioned reinforcer.

Sense-making and problem solving are usually highly beneficial activities. Solving problems is often necessary for people to achieve goals connected with values, for example. And in the area of romance, figuring out the best ways to meet potential love interests is an important problem that needs to be solved.

Despite the fact that seeking and achieving coherence is important and positive in many domains, this aspect of people's verbal learning history is not always a good thing. Sometimes, it can cut people off from their values. For example, consider the case of a man who discovers that he is infertile. Though his values might include an intimate relationship and a family, after receiving this news he might avoid dating, reasoning that he is now much less attractive to potential partners and will therefore have a much reduced chance of pairing up with someone with whom he might want to start a family. He may then cling to this relatively coherent description and offer it as an excuse for giving up dating. He may reason that life is unfair—that there are winners and losers and that he should resign himself to losing.

Apart from apparently providing a coherent excuse for avoiding dating, this description might also be reinforcing simply by virtue of being coherent, both internally as well as with regard to well-established relational networks concerning sex and attraction, success and failure, and perhaps such ideals as stoicism. Coherence is a powerful conditioned reinforcer, and thus it feels good to attain it. However, in the long run, acting in accordance with one's values (i.e., in this case, continuing to date) is likely to be more fulfilling than simply feeling "right."

Deictic Relational Framing

One key type of relational framing is *deictic framing* (the word "deictic" means "depending on the point of view of the speaker"), which provides verbal references to subject, space, and time. RFT sees deictic framing as underlying perspective-taking ability and individuals' development of a self-concept. The three key deictic frames are I-YOU, HERE-THERE, and NOW-THEN (see, e.g., Hayes, 1984). According to D. Barnes-Holmes, Hayes, and Dymond (2001, p. 122), "[a]bstraction of an individual's perspective on the world, and that of others, requires a combination of a sufficiently well-developed relational repertoire and an extensive history of multiple exemplars that take advantage of that repertoire." In other words, the individual first needs to learn to relationally frame the objects, people, and events in his or her current experience and then, in order to learn to acquire appropriate perspective on that experience, needs multiple opportunities to respond appropriately in accordance with the deictic cues that people in his or her social environment use with respect to that experience. In the course of interactions with the verbal community, a child will gradually learn to appropriately respond to and ask such questions as "What are you doing here?" "What am I doing now?" and "What will you do there?" The physical environment in which such questions are asked and answered will differ across exemplars, but the required relational patterns of I-YOU, HERE-THERE, and NOW-THEN will be consistent; thus, as in the case of the learning of other relational frames, these patterns will be abstracted over time (see, e.g., McHugh, Barnes-Holmes, & Barnes-Holmes, 2004).

According to RFT, once one establishes the deictic frames of I-YOU, HERE-THERE, and NOW-THEN in his or her behavioral repertoire, they become an inherent property of most verbal events. In this account, whenever one talks to another person, it is from the perspective of I, located HERE and NOW, about events occurring THERE (i.e., another place) and very often both THERE and THEN (i.e., another place and time). Even in the simple greeting "How are you?" the speaker is typically asking HERE and NOW about the situation of YOU (the listener) located THERE (wherever the listener is) and THEN (when the greeting is heard). The same analysis applies to situations in which one talks to oneself. If I criticize myself with the statement "That was stupid" after making a mistake, then I, HERE and NOW, am judging myself THERE and THEN (where and when I made the error). In summary, deictic frames establish a constant division between the speaker, who is always HERE and NOW, and whatever he or she is speaking about, which is THERE and (very typically also) THEN.

The Three Verbal Selves

RFT also suggests that, in combination with an extended relational repertoire, perspective-taking can establish three functionally different types of (verbal) self: (i) self as the *content* of verbal relations; (ii) self as an *ongoing process* of verbal relations; and (iii) self as the *context* of verbal relations (Hayes, 1995).

Self-as-Content

Self-as-content, or the conceptualized self, consists of elaborate descriptive and evaluative relational networks that people, over time, construct about themselves and their individual history. As soon as children become self-aware, they begin to interpret, explain, evaluate, predict, and rationalize their behavior. They organize these descriptions and evaluations of their own history and tendencies into a coherent network, a consistent presentation of a "self" that generally persists across time and situations.

Self-evaluations are always made HERE and NOW about behaviors that occur THERE and THEN. However, rarely is this process of interpreting and evaluating attended to as it happens in the present moment. Difficulties occur when products of relational responding (e.g., thoughts, judgments, comparisons, and beliefs) are treated as objectively true and inherent aspects of the real world, a process referred to within acceptance and commitment therapy as *cognitive fusion*. Cognitive fusion can be problematic when self-evaluations come to appear as historically rooted and unchangeable; self-stories (stories about who one is and how one came to be that way) may ossify and no longer simply describe past behavior, but also guide future behavior in directions that maintain the coherence of a story. This may result in ignoring or discounting evidence that contradicts the story, selectively attending to and amplifying confirmatory evidence, and acting in ways that are consistent with the story.

Self-as-Process

Self-as-process, or the knowing self, is the ongoing verbal discrimination of internal (i.e., private; psychological) events or experiences as they occur. Statements that reflect the self as a process of knowing typically begin with such phrases as "I feel," "I think," and "I wonder." The knowing self feeds the conceptualized self (e.g., in order to know that "I am a depressed person," I must first know that I frequently feel sad and have low energy across many contexts) and is also necessary to contact a transcendent sense of self-as-context, since a self-monitoring repertoire is required to observe the observer.

Self-as-process is critical to human psychological development. In order to respond effectively to his or her own responding, one must first be aware of how one is responding and the effect that it is having. For example, understanding and responding to one's thoughts and feelings about other people's behavior in a fluid and flexible manner is critical in personal relationships. This is particularly the case for romantic relationships, in which so much of one's intimate emotional life is shared with another.

The knowing self is extremely useful in behavioral regulation not only for the individual, but also for other members of the verbal community. Statements made from the knowing self allow people to predict an individual's behavior without knowledge of that person's learning history. For example, if Mary says that she feels anger toward Joe, this may allow other people to then predict how Mary might act toward Joe in particular contexts.

Self-as-Context

Self-as-context is the constant in all self-discriminations. If you answer many different questions about yourself and your behavior, the only aspect of your answering that will be consistent across time is the context from which the answer is given—that is, I, HERE and NOW. As such, it has been described as the "coming together and flexible social extension of deictic framing—especially I/here/now—to enable observation or description from a point of view," and has been said to enable or facilitate "a wide variety of experiences, including defusion, acceptance, compassion, empathy, theory of mind, and a transcendent sense of self" (Hayes, 2011).

Self-as-context has important implications for changing the way people experience and regulate psychological pain, since this sense of self cannot be threatened by aversive content in the way that the conceptualized or knowing self can. It allows people to confront deep emotional pain and facilitates willingness, compassion, and intimacy.

The Verbal Other

The concept of the verbal other is especially relevant in relationships. The verbal other is analogous to the verbal self in important respects, including the notion that, just as perspective-taking can establish three functionally distinct types of self, it can establish three distinct types of other—namely, other as *stable content*; other as *ongoing experiential process*; and other as *the context of verbal relations* (Hayes, 1995).

The conceptualized other is a verbal construction of another person with whom we are interacting. For example, I might assume different things about a new acquaintance whom I had previously been told held strongly religious beliefs than one whom I had been told was an atheist and might approach a conversation with the person differently on that basis; in other words, I might verbally construct a different listener, producing a different pattern of transformations of function for me as a speaker.

Other-as-process, or the knowing other, is also a verbal construction, but a more fluid one because in this case, one constructs the reactions of another on a moment-by-moment basis. This tends to happen in conversations as one verbally constructs how the other person is reacting to what one has said, and it is especially characteris¬tic of more personal conversations in which the other person is likely to disclose feelings (e.g., "I'm a little disappointed to hear you say that").

The other-as-context refers to the perspective of another person. As previously suggested, when referring to the self, perspective is created based on the "coming together and flexible social extension of deictic framing—especially I/here/now—to enable observation and description from a point of view" (Hayes, 2011). The greater the extent to which we can understand and experience someone else's situation on an ongoing basis (i.e., derive and undergo transformations of functions in accordance with deictic relations with respect to that person), the greater the extent to which we can contact the other-as-context and build up an appreciation of that other person's experience.

What becomes clear is that one important concept related to the verbal other is that of empathy. And the key process underlying empathy from the RFT point of view is transformation of emotional functions through deictic relations. So, for example, if you have just experienced an emotionally traumatic event, and another person takes your perspective through deictic framing (e.g., "If I were you…"), then that person may experience your emotional state through transformation of functions via the I-YOU frame. This conception of empathy is obviously pertinent to the "other-as-process" described above; for instance, a committed therapist listening to a client describe his or her current experience in the therapeutic context will likely deictically frame the client's experience and thus share that experience to an important extent. This concept of empathy is also obviously relevant to the other-as-context. In this case, the more contact one has with aspects of the other person's experience over time, the greater the understanding and appreciation that one will have of that person's perspective on the world. These are obviously key processes in intimate relationships. Ideally, a romantic relationship involves sharing intimate emotional experiences. The process of transformation of emotional functions through deictic relations is the RFT conception of how sharing of such experiences literally occurs.

Rule-Governed Behavior

In addition to facilitating the functional analysis of perspective-taking, and of self versus other, RFT provides new insight on rule-governed behavior and associated phenomena, which are critically important in understanding complex human behavior. Let us first briefly discuss rule-governed behavior and associated effects and then consider the RFT analysis of these phenomena.

Whereas nonhumans learn primarily through respondent and operant conditioning, humans (provided they have learned a language) are profoundly affected by rules specifying how they should behave. These rules are generated sometimes by other people (e.g., "You need to get out more often") and sometimes from within (self-rules; e.g., "I need to get out more often"). Note that the concept of "rules" as used within behavior analysis and RFT is broader than the conventional sense of "rule" as a verbal statement that prescribes behavior (e.g., "Keep off the grass"); "rule" as used by behavior analysis and RFT refers to verbal statements about the world that can influence behavior more generally. For example, the statement "I am unattractive" would be considered a rule, because it can change the way in which the person who thinks it or speaks it interacts with other people.

Rule-following can be extremely advantageous. For instance, research shows that rule-following facilitates people's adaptation to their environment better than operant contingency shaping alone (e.g., Ayllon & Azrin, 1964; Baron, Kaufman, & Stauber,

1969; Weiner, 1970). For example, you could learn a sequence of actions in a game much more quickly by having the sequence described to you than by trial and error. In addition, rules can bring about certain behaviors (e.g., the repertoire of behavior needed to play a complex card game, such as bridge) with much more precision than contingency shaping, and they can also bring behavior under the control of greatly delayed consequences (e.g., "Study hard and you'll succeed in your career").

While rules can help people navigate their world more effectively, we also know that human behavior can come under the influence of rules to the exclusion of other sources of environmental control (e.g., Kaufman, Baron, & Kopp, 1966). Consider a man who, after a number of romantic rejections, generates the rule "I am fundamentally unlovable." He might subsequently act according to this rule by giving up dating and resigning himself to a single life. If he had continued to date, despite emotionally painful episodes, he might eventually have met someone with whom he could enjoy a stable relationship. However, behaving in accordance with the rule prevents him from ever finding out. Much basic empirical work has documented this phenomenon of rule-based insensitivity to contingencies, wherein people under the influence of a rule are much less likely to adapt to changes in their environment (e.g., Hayes, Brownstein, Haas, & Greenway, 1986; Matthews, Shimoff, Catania, & Sagvolden, 1977; Shimoff, Catania, & Matthews, 1981; see Hayes, 1989, for an overview).

A Functional Analysis of Rules

Despite the apparent importance of rules and rule-governed behavior, for a long time there was no adequate functional analysis of these phenomena in Western psychology, because there was no adequate functional analytic theory of language. This has now changed with the advent of relational frame theory.

Skinner (1966) defined rules as contingency-specifying stimuli, but he failed to define the key term "specify" in behavior analytic terms. The RFT approach now allows us to define specification in terms of transformation of stimulus functions through arbitrarily applicable relations. More specifically, RFT provides an analysis of rule-governed behavior in terms of the relational frames involved and the cues that occasion the derivation of those relations, and also in terms of the psychological functions transformed through those relations and the cues that occasion those transformations of function (e.g., D. Barnes-Holmes et al., 2001).

Consider the statement "Stand outside the entrance to the cinema at 7:15, and I'll meet you there." This rule specifies spatial and temporal antecedents, the form and context of the response, and the nature of the consequence. From an RFT perspective, it involves the following specific relational frames: *coordination* between words (e.g., "cinema") and actual objects or events; *before-after* relations (the word "and" indicates a temporal antecedent); and *deictic* (perspective-taking) relations based on the cues "I," "you" (implied), and "there." With respect to transformation of stimulus functions, the words "stand outside" alter the behavioral functions of the cinema such that the listener is more likely to stand near it in the context specified in the rule (i.e., at 7:15).

It may seem self-evident that people are able to evaluate whether they are following a rule, but it is important to explain this in RFT terms: a person provided with a rule for behavior can determine whether he or she is following the rule by the extent to which the rule coordinates with his or her actual behavior. More technically, for the rule follower, the coordination between the relational network constituted by the rule and the relations sustained among the objects or events specified by the rule act as an ongoing source of behavioral regulation. In other words, if the person sees that events in the environment specified by the rule are indeed in the relations specified by the rule, then the rule is being followed. In the example just given, if you (as the listener) see that you are standing outside the cinema when your watch shows 7:15, then you are following the rule.

Functional Categories of Rules

Zettle and Hayes (1982) suggested three functionally different categories of rule-following: *pliance, tracking,* and *augmenting.* In each case, the process we just outlined—deriving a relation of coordination between a rule and one's behavior—occurs; however, an additional pattern determines the behavioral effect.

Pliance is rule-governed behavior under the control of socially mediated reinforcement for following rules; an example is little Jimmy's following his mother's rule about tidying his room because his previous rule-following has resulted in praise and attention or avoidance of punishment.

Tracking is rule-governed behavior under the control of a history of coordination between rules and the arrangement of the environment independent of the delivery of those rules; an example is a student's following a rule provided by a teacher about which textbook sections to read for an upcoming exam because following rules delivered by teachers has allowed the student to succeed in school; this success was not directly arranged by teachers in order to reinforce following of the rule, but was simply a consequence of more effective studying.

Augmenting is rule-governed behavior due to relational networks that alter the degree to which events function as consequences. There are two forms of augmenting: formative and motivative. *Formative* augmenting generates consequential functions for a previously neutral stimulus; for instance, being told in the context of a game that blue tokens are worth points makes gaining blue tokens reinforcing in that context. *Motivative* augmenting changes the effectiveness of a stimulus already functioning as a consequence. For example, you might already like the taste of chocolate, but seeing an ad that describes how good chocolate tastes might make you even more likely to buy it the next time you go shopping. One way of explaining the effect of such rules is that they function as verbal counterparts to the nonverbal behavioral effect of *reinforcer sampling*, an establishing or motivative operation whereby organisms exposed to particular types of reinforcers (e.g., food) subsequently work harder for those reinforcers. Motivative augmental rules may work by presenting the functions of reinforcers verbally rather than physically (i.e., via transformation of stimulus functions).

Self-Rules

In addition to the analysis of rules provided by others, RFT allows for the analysis of self-rules, which depends to some extent on the analysis of self that we have discussed. Self-rules are an important topic, because people may produce vast numbers of self-rules that guide their behavior every day. Some of these rules are simple and trivial (e.g., "I should give Mary a call"), while others are complex and profound (e.g., "I must propose marriage in a way that is romantic and memorable");

however, their effect is undoubtedly significant. Self-rules are relevant with respect to both self-as-content and self-as-process. In regard to self-as-content, for example, you may prescribe a rule for yourself based on your concept of yourself (e.g., "I won't bother asking him out on a date because I'm too shy"). However, self-rules produced on the basis of self-as-process are particularly important, because they guide behavior in an ongoing way in potentially important situations. Such rules might include the appropriate way to act in the presence of particular feelings in particular contexts (e.g., affection with an intimate other) and may be relatively useful (e.g., by encouraging allowance of deep feelings) or potentially disadvantageous (e.g., by encouraging avoidance of deep feelings).

Another important distinction is between *strategic* and *valuative* self-rules. The first refers to strategic behavior that tends to occur relatively soon after the rule is made; for example, "I have to get to the restaurant by seven tonight." Valuative self-rules, on the other hand, explicitly refer to longer-term valued objectives that are more overarching. An example in this case is "I'd like a more intimate relationship with my partner." In strategic self-rules, the behavioral terms specified tend to have relatively precise functions. In the case given above, for instance, both the behavior involved ("getting to the restaurant") and the antecedent conditions ("by seven") are clearly defined. In valuative self-rules, the functions of the terms involved tend not to be as well specified. For example, the meaning of the term "a more intimate relationship" is more complex than that of "getting to the restaurant by seven." Furthermore, the nature of the behavior required is also much less obvious than in the case of the first rule.

Valuative self-rules may be analyzed as motivative augmental rules. They function to augment the reinforcing functions of a valued direction. Value statements, such as "I'd like a more intimate relationship with my partner," are relatively complex in terms of the relational network and the reinforcement involved, but they essentially work the same as other, simpler motivative augmental rules, such as the one above involving chocolate. Words and phrases like "more intimate" present some of the emotional, sensory, and perceptual functions of greater intimacy and therefore tend to increase the likelihood of behavior that works to produce this consequence.

RFT and Verbal Love: Preview

Relational framing is the core of language (i.e., verbal behavior) and is what makes human behavior so different from—and human love and sexuality much more rich and complex than—that of other animals. In the previous chapter, we described basic behavioral processes that underlie the development of human love. These powerful processes, which shape and motivate people's erotic and affectionate behavior to a significant extent, are similar in other animals. However, with the unique capacity for verbal behavior, humans come to respond in ways different from other animals. Humans do not simply interact with their environment, as other animals do—once they have become proficient at relational framing, they interact with it verbally as well. Thus, all the processes discussed in the previous chapter can be fundamentally affected by the "verbal layer" of responding.

Before we advance any further in our focus on love and romance from an RFT perspective, one thing we might ask is whether we should try to define the terms "love," "romance," "intimacy," and "sexuality." After all, these terms seem to refer to phenomena of core importance in our discussion, and functional contextualist behavior analysis, including RFT, is an attempt to provide a newly scientific perspective on human activity connected with these terms. However, from an RFT point of view, these are lay terms, not technical psychological terms, and therefore there is no reason to either sharply define them or expect clear technical distinctions to overlap entirely with them. Such terms only orient us to particular domains of interest. RFT can describe and discuss technically definable phenomena (conditioning, relational framing, motivative augmental control, etc.) that occur within these domains, and this can be enough to allow us to construct a scientifically useful understanding of the patterns of behavior in which we are most interested.

Early Childhood

In the previous chapter, we discussed the fact that human beings, like other species, develop a strong bond with their caregivers at an early age. As the child-caregiver interaction becomes increasingly verbal, language processes can powerfully affect this bond. In many typical child-caregiver relationships, language can enrich the interaction and make it a greater source of reinforcement for both parties, and have a particularly powerful effect on the learning experience of the child. For example, imagine a caregiver and a child playing together and discussing what they are doing, the caregiver guiding and instructing the child. In such an interaction, language can boost the functions of the experience for the child by, for example, allowing him or her to experience verbal coherence (e.g., learning new interesting things, figuring things out) as well as jokes and stories provided by the caregiver. It can also directly provide powerful verbal reinforcement (e.g., "You're so smart, sweetheart—you've figured it out!"). In addition, language allows the positive relationship between child and caregiver itself to be described (e.g., "Mommy and Daddy love you"). Verbal activity can thus strengthen a loving child-caregiver relationship, and affect the child's experience in particular in powerful ways, laying the foundation for healthy adult relationships. At the same time, language can also amplify the negative aspects of a less than loving relationship and the negative dimensions of the experience for the child. An obvious example is a caregiver scolding a child and accusing the child of being bad or wicked. Consistent verbal interactions of this type might result in emotional pain and deep insecurity on the part of the child (e.g., the child has the thought, *I'm worthless*) that might make healthy emotional interactions with other people as he or she matures less likely.

Late Childhood

So far, we have described relatively simple ways in which language can affect the emotional life of a growing child. As the child grows, he or she gains in verbal ability and interacts with an increasingly complex verbal environment, and thus relationships with parents and others can become more complex. For example, as the child becomes more sophisticated in terms of perspective-taking ability (based on deictic relational framing), he or she can become more empathic and more sophisticated with regard to appropriate displays of affection. For instance, a girl might buy a particular present for her father based on her understanding of what he would like. The same girl, whose parents are separated, might come to realize that she should not talk about her father in glowing terms in front of her mother, even though both parents have assured her of their continuing love for and devotion to her. She might frame in this way: "If I were Mom, and I heard my daughter praise Dad, then I might wonder whether she preferred him to me, and so I might feel hurt or angry." Such a consideration might involve making multiple distinctions, including between I and YOU (i.e., Mom), between HERE and THERE (e.g., a situation in which I might praise Dad), and between NOW and THEN (e.g., a time when I praise Dad in front of Mom).

Sexual Maturity

With the advent of sexual maturity and interactions with potential romantic partners, the verbal dimension of interactions—including perspective-taking relations in particular—becomes very important. Human verbal ability allows for a unique level of complexity and experiential richness in relationships.

One obvious example of how verbal behavior can enrich and complexify human sexual relationships is the concept of romance. The modern Western concept of romantic love between two people (initially and still stereotypically involving a man and a woman, but recently admitting same-sex couples) prescribes romantic symbols (e.g., wedding rings; love hearts; Venice, Italy; Eros/Cupid; and Aphrodite/Venus), stories (e.g., romantic novels and romantic comedies), and traditions (e.g., Valentine's Day); it prescribes aspects of courtship and dating rituals (e.g., buying the other person flowers or chocolates) and normative pair-bonding rituals (e.g., engagement party and wedding ceremony); and it sets standards of achievement to which people are expected to aspire (e.g., maintenance of a life-long monogamous relationship, preferably one that produces children). These features are all well-known elements of Western culture that are communicated to each new generation and transform the functions of children's relational networks concerning themselves, others, and the social world in which they participate. Young people's interactions with peers, especially those to whom they are sexually attracted, are likely shaped by these stories to at least some extent.

For example, a young man who asks the object of his desire out on a date might have expectations concerning how he and the other person should behave on the date that conform somewhat with relevant socially accepted norms regarding dating. If the norms of dating are violated (for example, if the other person abruptly ends the date) or the date ends conventionally but in a way that the young man interprets as signaling rejection (for instance, his date seems bored or at least less eager than he is), then the date may be a profoundly negative experience. For instance, derivation of such relations as "I'm not good enough" or "I'm unlovable," with accompanying transformation of negative emotional functions, may make the experience particularly aversive. On the other hand, if the date goes well, then for hours afterward the young man may reminisce about it while imagining details of possible future dates and of an extended relationship.

Hence, verbal behavior makes affectionate and erotic aspects of human relationships considerably complex and experientially powerful (see also Roche & Barnes, 1997, for discussion of how relational framing can affect sexuality in particular).

One of the advantages of RFT is that it gives us the tools to conceptualize and explore the potential complexity of human relationships in some detail. RFT also facilitates insight into what can go wrong with relationships and what might be done to help them. This latter contribution is influenced too by acceptance and commitment therapy (ACT), an approach to psychotherapy inspired by the same functional contextualist approach to human language as RFT. In the next chapter, we examine ACT in detail. Beginning in chapter 5, we explore the ACT/RFT approach to love and romantic relationships in detail.

Summary

In this chapter, we introduced and provided some key theoretical details of relational frame theory (RFT), the behavior analytic approach to language and cognition that underlies the theoretical analysis of human love and sexuality provided in this book. RFT sees language and cognition as *relational framing*, an operant ability that develops through exposure to verbal interactions, takes multiple forms, and is characterized by mutual entailment, combinatorial entailment, and transformation of stimulus functions. We discussed several central aspects of human psychology—including bidirectional stimulus relations, relational coherence, deictic (perspective-taking) relations, and rule-governed behavior—that are extrapolations and extensions from the basic analysis, and will be important in our discussion of acceptance and commitment therapy (ACT) in the next chapter and in the ACT/RFT exploration of romance and love later on. We suggested that verbal ability is hugely important with respect to the character of human love and sexuality, and we indicated briefly how it might influence these—hinting at ideas that we explore in more detail ahead. Finally, we suggested that verbal ability is hugely important with respect to relationships and the development of intimacy, which form the basis of love. We explore these concepts in more detail later in the book.

CHAPTER 4

Acceptance and Commitment Therapy

Introduction

In the previous chapter, we discussed the basics of relational frame theory, which is the application of behavior analytic science to language and cognition. In the current chapter, we explore acceptance and commitment therapy (ACT), an approach to psychological functioning that follows the relational frame theory (RFT) conception of human language and suggests how human functioning might be optimized in accordance with this understanding.

Many of the effects of language (i.e., relational framing) are profoundly positive. At an individual level, language helps people think, problem solve, and plan for the future; at a societal level, it enables tremendous cultural and technical progress. With respect to human love and sexuality, language enables people to experience deeply intimate and meaningful relationships. At the same time, however, language can dominate people's behavior to such an extent that it cuts them off from psychologically optimal courses of action. With respect to relationships, language can lead to behavior that deprives people of opportunities to connect with others or to experience human love as fully and openly as possible.

The key purpose of acceptance and commitment therapy is to address and overcome these negative effects of language/relational framing and to facilitate maximum psychological flexibility. When it comes to guiding psychologically healthy behavior, ACT is, of course, as relevant to loving and sexual relationships as it is to other areas of human behavior, and we use aspects of the ACT framework to discuss key issues in love and relationships in later chapters of this book. Before we do that, however, we first have to explain the processes involved in ACT. We explain these processes primarily in relatively nontechnical language, and we continue to use that level of language, for the most part, for the rest of the book. In this chapter, however, since an important aim of this book is to demonstrate our approach's connection to basic science, we provide a more explicitly RFT-based interpretation of each process.

The processes important in ACT are acceptance, defusion, self-as-context, present awareness, values, and committed action. These six processes can also be thought of as three pairs of complementary processes—namely, acceptance and defusion, self-as-context and present awareness, and values and committed action. Let us examine these processes from an RFT perspective, with a special emphasis on their relevance to relationships and sexuality.

Acceptance and Defusion

The complementary processes of acceptance and defusion can help people respond in a more psychologically healthy way to their own thoughts and feelings. This type of responding can prevent people from reacting to particular experiences in relationships in ways that could work to undermine those relationships.

Acceptance

In order to characterize acceptance, let us begin with its inverse: experiential avoidance. Experiential avoidance (introduced in chapter 3) refers to attempts to control, alter, or escape from private (i.e., internal; psychological) events or experiences—thoughts, feelings, or sensations—even when attempts to do so can cause psychological harm (Hayes, Wilson, Gifford, Follette, & Strosahl, 1996).

The ability to predict and avoid aversive situations involving fear, pain, rejection, and isolation is important for human survival, and historically it has served humans well. By avoiding large, fearsome animals, for example, our ancestors were more likely to survive and reproduce. However, the human capacity for language enables a type of avoidance that can be severely maladaptive. People's capacity to relationally frame and formulate rules regarding their experiences, which was described in the previous chapter, can enable unhelpful transformation of stimulus functions of an experience such that they attempt to escape or avoid that experience even when it is not helpful to do so. For instance, you might formulate the rule that anxiety is unpleasant and you need to get rid of your anxiety before you can live a full and vital life. (Indeed, many people do formulate a rule like this one.) This rule will likely transform the functions of your anxiety such that you will act to avoid your anxiety. However, as empirical evidence indicates, anxiety and other emotional experiences cannot be easily controlled in this way, and your avoidant behavior will likely only move you away from the full and vital life you desire.

The domain of intimate relationships is often linked with experiences that might be evaluated as negative and needing to be controlled. Every intimate relationship entails emotional ups and downs—periods when attraction is strong, and moments of rejection—there is time together, and there is time apart. There are innumerable physical and psychological experiences that people are likely to evaluate as unwanted and uncomfortable—even threatening or harmful—in an intimate relationship. Most people are likely to use whatever coping skills they have learned to try to avoid these negative feelings, thoughts, memories, or sensations.

From an ACT perspective, we would say that a behavior has the function of experiential avoidance if it occurs when the threat is only verbally derived as opposed to actually present in the nonverbal (i.e., physical) environment. In other words, people avoid a situation or experience when they tell themselves there is a threat, or when they perceive a threat, despite the fact that there is none. For example, a boy who is sexually molested might develop an adaptive strategy of "shutting down" or disassociating feelings, thoughts, and physical sensations in encounters of this nature. This avoidance of the nonverbal threat is adaptive. However, the boy might derive a rule about sex in general being dangerous and threatening and, hence, later, as a man, might have problems relaxing while having sex with his partner. In this case, the context might have changed in key respects, but as a result of transformation of functions via the rule, the avoidant behavior remains the same. The problematic results of experiential avoidance are immediately obvious in this case, because the man and his partner will have less satisfying sex than they might otherwise and the relationship will likely suffer. Such problems might play a role in bringing about the end of the relationship. If this becomes a pattern in the man's relationships, and he subsequently derives the rule that all his relationships inevitably end in emotional pain and rejection, he may begin to avoid getting into relationships at all, thus shutting down a very important potential source of satisfaction and meaning in life.

Other kinds of avoidance in relationships may seem less problematic when they first arise than in the example above. For example, Kristal might start avoiding engaging with her partner on a particular topic because the two have fought about that topic in the past. Avoidance of a potentially heated exchange or of other emotionally undesirable experiences may seem like a good thing in the short term. However, in the long term, it is likely to be problematic, because Kristal's sensitivity to these unwanted experiences is likely to increase, and she may engage in larger and larger patterns of avoidance and escape in order to remain out of contact with them. For example, she may start to avoid other topics also, resulting in less communication with her partner more generally, with the result that the relationship suffers. Furthermore, experiential avoidance as a rigid, pervasive pattern of behavior can lead to excessive narrowing of options as it cultivates unwillingness to experience discomfort on ever smaller levels.

The alternative to experiential avoidance is *acceptance*. Acceptance in the ACT sense primarily refers to behavior, rather than a belief or state of mind, and involves the active and aware embrace of private events without attempting to change their frequency or form. From a more technical RFT point of view, acceptance can be interpreted as following a rule that specifies contacting the automatic stimulus functions of psychological events without acting to avoid or change those functions (e.g., Hayes, 1994). From an ACT perspective, no matter how negative any private experience might seem, it is only when one holds this mental content in a specific context that it will be psychologically harmful. Acceptance implies changing not the *nature* of private events but one's own *willingness* to experience those events. The full spectrum of thoughts, feelings, and sensations— both positive and negative—is still present. The difference is that particular private events are embraced rather than avoided.

Consider what might happen if someone who avoided sexual intimacy due to aversive experiences, such as the man in the example above, tried acceptance instead. Acceptance in this case might involve deliberately entering into an intimate relationship; during the development of that relationship, deliberately entering into situations in which intimacy was a possibility;

and in the context of intimacy, allowing previously avoided memories, feelings, thoughts, and physical sensations to arise and be experienced. The consequence of this kind of acceptance of internal events is that, through exposure, the events themselves become less aversive, and, of course, that the person is potentially able to garner all the positive things that can come from being in a relationship.

With regard to acceptance, it is important to note that we are referring not just to events perceived as negative, but also to those perceived as positive. Accepting reality as it is, rather than as one would like it to be, can be difficult. Just as people have a tendency to want to avoid events they deem negative, they also have a tendency to cling to and repeat those they deem positive. For example, in the early stage of their relationship, a couple may experience a euphoric feeling while having sex; yet, over time, the ecstatic feelings may lessen. One or both partners may then long for things to be the way they were and may even start chasing that feeling while disregarding the reality of the present moment. Chasing the feeling can lead to chasing a new lover and throwing away a valued relationship. Attempting to recreate a private event takes one away from the present moment as much as attempting to avoid doing so does. Understanding the transitory nature of private events is important to acceptance. Acceptance means seeing the transitory nature of all forms as we know them. Any feeling, no matter how difficult or painful it is, or how wonderful it is, will rise and fall.

Defusion

Acceptance is facilitated by the process of cognitive *defusion*. Again, let us start with the inverse of the term concerned. The

79

inverse of cognitive defusion is cognitive *fusion*, which is when people experience thoughts as literal truths and, as such, something to which they must respond. In RFT terms, fusion could be understood to involve a transformation of functions such that people respond in accordance with the literal meaning of their relational framing (i.e., they "buy into" their thoughts).

Fusion is a product of years of immersion in a socio-verbal culture. It greatly facilitates participation in and cooperation within society and thus can often be a positive thing. For example, when children buy into the rules given to them by their parents (e.g., "Don't talk to strangers") and respond on the basis of those rules, they will likely avoid genuine threats. On the other hand, though, fusion can also be a negative phenomenon. For example, if you buy into the self-evaluation "I'm not good enough," you may stop trying to achieve things in life that matter to you, and as a result you may lose out on a lot of what life has to offer. It is fusion in this negative, problematic sense with which ACT is concerned and which we are mainly referring to in what follows.

With regard to relationships, fusion can create much suffering. Fusion might prevent someone from establishing a relationship in the first place. For example, someone might think, *I am unlovable*, and might respond to this thought not simply as an idiosyncratic reaction to certain experiences but as literal truth, subsequently avoiding intimate relationships, because any relationship is seen as certain to fail.

Fusion can also create suffering within relationships. For example, imagine that Bailey has an idea about what love is and how someone who "loves" another should act toward him or her. This idea that Bailey has created as the "truth" will be the yardstick she uses when attempting to establish and maintain intimate relationships. For example, perhaps she expects that her partner should show her his love by repeatedly telling her how much he loves her. However, her partner has a different idea of what love looks like. For example, he sees love as being about small, subtle gestures of affection. When he shows his love in his way, it isn't in accordance with Bailey's conception of what love is about. Since Bailey regards her picture of love as a literal truth, it takes her away from the actual loving behavior being directed toward her at this moment—her mental picture seems more real than the actual present moment—and she concludes that her partner doesn't love her.

In addition, fusion may lead to a way of life governed by a constant need to respond to private experiences at the expense of responding to the outer world. For instance, in the example just given, when Bailey's partner does not behave the way she expects, perhaps she starts to have feelings of uncertainty in the relationship. She might then respond to these feelings by seeking reassurance from her partner that she is loved. She might begin to organize her overt behavior to try to reduce the form and frequency of these feelings and any related thoughts. However, the more energy she invests in trying to manage her thoughts and feelings, the less flexible her behavior will be and the less likely it is that she will be living in accordance with her values.

Cognitive fusion and experiential avoidance are intertwined. The more that people negatively evaluate their private experiences, and the more fused they become with them, the less willing they are to experience them. Fusion with evaluations about private experiences (e.g., "I don't like uncertainty") builds further unwillingness. People who are feeling insecure in a relationship are likely to say, "I don't want to feel insecure," and to look for ways to get rid of that feeling. Since these thoughts are taken as literal truths, they necessitate management responses in order to escape the situation. When people take the stance that private experiences are causal and threatening, patterns of experiential avoidance increase. For example, Bailey may believe that the insecurity that she feels in her relationship is "caused" by her partner's behavior, and she may respond by trying to control her partner's behavior. Her partner is likely to resist, however, which, in turn, will trigger more feelings of uncertainty in Bailey. Hence a vicious cycle ensues.

The solution to cognitive fusion is cognitive defusion. At its core, this is a process in which people come to experience thoughts as simply thoughts—as fleeting events that they need not directly respond to, challenge, or control. For example, imagine having the thought *My partner is being unfaithful.* Fusion with this thought would involve treating it as the literal truth and responding accordingly, perhaps by acting with jealousy and starting a fight. Defusion, on the other hand, would involve responding to it as simply a fleeting verbal event that is not the same as a truth and does not necessitate a response.

Human beings, with their history of immersion in language and responding in accordance with language, are very prone to fusion and do not engage in much spontaneous defusion. However, ACT sees defusion as an important skill that people can learn in support of their own psychological health, and ACT practitioners teach a number of techniques to facilitate defusion. One such technique is the "leaves on a river" visualization or meditation, in which one imagines putting each of his or her thoughts on leaves floating down a river. This allows one to get some perspective on these thoughts and to see them as thoughts, rather than getting "caught up" in them and acting on them.

Another technique is to repeat words or phrases until they begin to lose their literal meaning. The typical example used is the word "milk." By repeating this word out loud over and over again ("milk," "milk," "milk"), one starts to experience it as only a sound rather than a meaningful word, and thus the literal meaning is undermined. Both of these techniques can be used for each and every thought, but, of course, they are particularly effective as therapeutic techniques when it comes to negative or troubling thoughts. In cognitive defusion, the thought *I am unlovable*, for example, might be reacted to as simply a thought and thus might less likely occasion unhelpful avoidance.

Defusion works in tandem with acceptance. As stated above, acceptance can be seen as following a rule that specifies contacting the automatic stimulus functions of psychological events without acting to avoid or change those functions. Again, no matter how negative any private experience might seem, it is only when one holds this mental content in a specific context that it will be psychologically harmful. This context is one of cognitive fusion, in which, as explained, there is transformation of functions such that people respond in accordance with the literal meaning of their relational framing (i.e., they "buy into" their thoughts). Defusion, on the other hand, has been interpreted as a process of changing contextual control to make unhelpful transformation of functions in accordance with verbally described experiences less likely (see, e.g., Blackledge, 2007). Imagining seeing thoughts as leaves floating down a river and hearing those thoughts said out loud over and over are both examples of contexts in which there may be less transformation of functions and thus less possibility of problematic responding.

Hence, cognitive defusion techniques work by altering the undesirable functions of thoughts, rather than trying to alter their form, their frequency, or the contexts that occasion them. The aim of these techniques is to reduce the dominance of the literal functions of private experiences by creating or strengthening alternative responses to such experiences. The result of defusion exercises is usually a decrease in the believability of or attachment to thoughts or other private events, rather than an immediate change in their frequency. For example, Marco often wonders whether his partner is cheating on him. After practicing defusing from thoughts of his partner's infidelity, Marco still has such thoughts just as often, but the believability of these thoughts and hence the likelihood of his reacting to them decreases. Once he is able to recognize such thoughts as simply thoughts, he spends less time struggling with these thoughts and has more time and energy to direct toward his values—both relationship centered and otherwise. In fact, values and the actions that move one toward them are key theoretical pillars of ACT, and thus it is to these that we turn next.

Values and Committed Action

Values provide the overarching directions for our lives, while *committed actions* are the behaviors that take us in those directions. Relationships with lovers, family, and friends are often key sources of values in people's lives. This is particularly true of intimate relationships, which can be a source of affection, sensual pleasure, companionship, and intellectual stimulation. In order to establish and maintain a stable relationship that offers these valued qualities, however, people must act in particular ways (i.e., engage in committed actions) that support such a relationship.

Values

Values are a core feature of the therapeutic process in ACT. In this context, they are defined as "freely chosen, verbally constructed consequences of ongoing, dynamic, evolving patterns of activity, which establish predominant reinforcers for that activity that are intrinsic in engagement in the valued behavioral pattern itself" (Wilson & Dufrene, 2009, p. 64). Let's examine this definition.

The first part describes values as freely chosen. "Free" in this case indicates the absence of aversive control. From a functional contextual perspective, neither free will nor determinism is ultimately (ontologically) "true"; however, people feel more free when they're acting to produce positive reinforcement for themselves than when they're trying to avoid or escape aversive situations (Skinner, 1971). For example, people likely feel freer when entering a relationship for the purpose of enriching their life than for the purpose of escaping or avoiding loneliness. From an ACT perspective, the feeling of making a free choice that comes from pursuing positive reinforcement rather than avoiding aversive stimuli is an important aspect of values.

The phrase "verbally constructed consequences" refers to the fact that values involve a linguistic conception of the consequences of valued action. For example, if you value intimacy in a relationship and are asked to describe what this value involves, you might say something like "being able to talk honestly and openly to someone else about my feelings and my experiences." This is a verbal construction or linguistic description based on your previous real-life experiences of intimacy, as well as extrapolations from or generalizations about some of the qualities of such experiences. Such verbally constructed consequences are a core part of what we mean by values, since they motivate people to act in particular ways (engage in valued actions) in order to achieve them.

The meaning of "ongoing, dynamic, evolving patterns of activity" is relatively straightforward. People engage in many different patterns of activity in their lifetimes, and some of these are particularly relevant to values in that they produce the kinds of verbally constructed consequences just discussed. For example, when people are seeking to initiate and establish the conditions for an intimate relationship, patterns of behavior that will be important include socializing, going on dates, identifying and reinforcing honesty within a burgeoning relationship, and opening up emotionally to someone at appropriate moments as the relationship develops. Over their lives, people may experience many dating situations and relationships; those experiences and their verbal descriptions of such will form ongoing, dynamic, evolving patterns of activity that may bring them closer to their verbally constructed values, which will also evolve over time and in accordance with their experiences. In other words, as people experience and describe dating and romantic situations, not only will their ideas about intimacy motivate continued engagement in such patterns of activity, those patterns will allow their verbal conception of intimacy to evolve to some extent, though the core idea of what intimacy involves (trust, honesty, closeness, etc.) will remain relatively constant.

In explaining the phrase "which establish predominant reinforcers," we should first note that basic, stable, and potentially long-term sources of reinforcement (e.g., affection, sensual stimulation, and social interaction) are very important in the ACT definition of values, since people value certain domains in their life primarily because these domains are related either directly or indirectly to these sources of reinforcement. For example, the rich tapestry of romantic stories, personal sexual history, and private understandings of self and other that are woven into most people's verbal constructions of what is involved in an "intimate relationship" ultimately receive their motivational power from their connections with such reinforcers as those just listed. The term "predominant" in the definition underlines the long-term central importance of these reinforcers.

Then we should clarify that the definition of values provided above is rooted in the RFT conceptualization of values as motivative augmental rules. Motivative augmental rules, as we explained in the last chapter, are verbal relational networks that serve to alter the degree to which previously established consequences function as reinforcers or, alternatively, punishers. Values are defined in terms of reinforcement rather than punishment, and thus values are verbal networks that alter the degree to which previously established consequences serve as reinforcers. More simply, they are ideas that serve to make particular consequences even more motivating. For example, when someone who values intimacy thinks about or is reminded of intimacy, that verbal reminder might produce an increased desire for intimate conversation or physical intimacy. That might make it more likely, in turn, that he or she will engage in the kinds of activities that can maintain intimacy (e.g., emotional honesty) or those that can eventually result in intimacy (e.g., dating), depending on the situation.

The final phrase in Wilson and Dufrene's definition of values is "intrinsic in engagement in the valued behavioral pattern." This is an elaborate description of the predominant reinforcers mentioned in the previous paragraph. This phrase simply suggests that these predominant or typical reinforcers are ones that are inherent in certain types of behavior. The word "intrinsic" highlights the fact that the reinforcers resulting from certain patterns of values-committed action, which are likely to have increased motivational power, are typical, natural, or sustainable, as opposed to atypical, artificial, or short term. Returning to the example of intimacy in relationships, intrinsic reinforcers include social acceptance, emotional support, physical touch, and sexual arousal. Each of these reinforcers is a typical and natural aspect of an intimate relationship, and, as such, might also be expected to be sustainable for as long as the relationship lasts.

In addition to this basic definition of values from an ACT perspective, values have a number of additional qualities that we should mention.

Values develop within a socio-verbal context. Although values are personal, they are shaped in part by what other people think of as good or bad, important or unimportant, and desirable or undesirable. As children grow, their community teaches them to describe what they want (hopefully accurately). Their parents introduce them to "appropriate" playmates and potential friends. Media and the commercial world present them with attractive dolls and animated figures and films, which form their ideas of what is attractive. Over time, they develop statements about what they want, their purpose, and a direction for their life. They develop images and statements about the perfect partner.

Values can never be completely attained, as they are defined within ACT as chosen, verbally constructed consequences that, rather than being fulfilled, function as motivation for certain behavioral directions. For example, a value of being a caring person in an intimate relationship can never be fulfilled. Even if the person gets married (a concrete goal), it would be silly to say, "Now that I'm married, I've accomplished caring, so I can move on to the next thing." Caring as a value is based on such behaviors as sharing personal information, taking an active interest, and anticipating a partner's wishes, none of which are about fulfilling concrete goals; they're behaviors in the direction of the value.

Values are technically rules and, thus, like other rules, might be responded to relatively rigidly (e.g., as statements of truth to which we must adhere at all costs). However, values are freely chosen and do not prescribe any particular behavior. In other words, if you value being nurturing in relationships, this rule of being nurturing does not indicate precisely how, with whom (or what), or how often you should engage in nurturing behaviors. Values as rules simply orient people to general patterns of purposeful behavior that will ideally be meaningful and reinforcing. People must learn how to choose particular behaviors that comport with those values by tracking the reinforcing consequences of their behavior. Hence, values give one a direction, but one must learn to monitor the course. Despite the connotation of a rule being rigid, flexibility is also important for living consistently with one's values. Even as the underlying value stays relatively the same, behaviors that embody that value may change in form over the years in response to different life circumstances. For example, a couple may not engage in as much sexual activity as they get older; however, perhaps they share other things to a greater extent instead, and, in either event, they may continue to value intimacy.

Committed Action

Committed action refers to behavior in accordance with extensive sets of concrete goals that are values consistent. As explained, from an RFT perspective, values are interpreted as the highest point in a relational network in which higher items on the network are enabled or facilitated by lower items (goals, sub-goals, etc.). An example of one such hierarchical relational network might have "intimacy" as its highest point, with, for example, "expressing emotion" and "spending time together" at lower points. Committed action is essentially responding in accordance with rules that prescribe action consistent with such a hierarchical network. For example, if Thomas is aware of the importance of "spending time together" as a goal that will facilitate greater contact with his partner, then he might formulate a rule prescribing a certain amount of weekly "quality time" together (e.g., "I'll put aside time every weekend"). If he subsequently acts consistently with this rule, he is demonstrating commitment to his value of "intimacy."

Not engaging in patterns of behavior that are consistent with their values can lead people to feel as if their life is meaningless or excessively painful. For example, after her partner of several years leaves her for another woman, Sheila is heartbroken. She decides that it's too painful to try to get into another relationship, and she throws herself into work and other commitments. However, despite continued enjoyment of and success in her career, she cannot deny that she is missing having someone special in her life. She contemplates the dating scene, but she feels awkward and unsure and still has painful memories of the breakup. She tells herself that things are going really well in her career and that she has no need to get into a relationship.

However, eventually even her career successes become tinged with pain, because they remind her that she has no one close with whom to share them.

In ACT, guiding the client in committed action in relation to his or her declared values is a key part of therapy. Protocols to produce committed action involve therapy work and home-work linked to short-term as well as long-term behavior-change goals. Behavior-change efforts, in turn, lead to contact with psychological barriers that are addressed through other ACT processes, such as acceptance and defusion. Therapist and client can map out small and large steps to encourage increasingly values-consistent behaviors. Taking steps in valued directions can make additional steps easier over time.

If a client values an intimate relationship, for example, but needs guidance in this respect, then the therapist might discuss the relevant steps of socializing, going on dates, identifying and reinforcing honesty within a burgeoning relationship, and opening up emotionally to the other person at appropriate moments as the relationship develops. Each of these steps, in turn, can be broken down into smaller steps. For example, socializing might require getting in contact with friends regularly and making sure to meet up and chat with them, and, given that this is a step toward establishing a relationship, outings to places where potential romantic partners might be found are important.

In addition, in the case of both values and committed action related to those values, some acceptance of the discomfort that might come from trying and failing at potentially important activities is part of the process. Going out with friends does not always lead to meeting eligible people; dating potential partners more often than not ends in disappointment; the honesty on the part of a partner that one might seek can be hurtful; and opening oneself up emotionally makes one vulnerable to emotional pain. Nevertheless, these steps toward intimacy are necessary in the pursuit of values in the domain of intimacy, and thus dealing with emotional discomfort is also a necessary part of the process.

Dealing with the emotional discomfort of pursuing values through committed action is facilitated by the skills of acceptance and defusion, which we have already discussed. The interplay between acceptance processes (acceptance and defusion) and values processes (values and committed action) that this illustrates is in fact the key dynamic within ACT—values provide people with the motivation to accept their experiences, while acceptance facilitates their behaving in accordance with their chosen values. However, in order to understand this dynamic more completely, we also need to understand the context in which it occurs: the behaving self.

Self-as-Context and Present Awareness

The self is the locus or context for all experiences, including values and valued activity as well as processes of acceptance and defusion that facilitate values-oriented behavior. Present awareness or mindfulness is a subset of self-activity in which people orient to their ongoing (moment-by-moment) experience so as to better facilitate both acceptance and values processes. With regard to relationships, a person's self-concept and how he or she relates to his or her ongoing experience in the context of the other person will affect the relationship and the experience of it in a fundamental way.

Self-as-Context

As explained in the previous chapter, relational frame theory explains the emergence of the self in terms of the verbal discrimination of one's own behavior from that of other people in accordance with deictic (perspective-taking) relations (I-YOU, HERE-THERE, and NOW-THEN). Responding in accordance with deictic relations allows one to discriminate a consistent locus of relational behavior such that I (i.e., as used, oneself) am always seen to be responding in the HERE and NOW, whereas YOU (another person, or other people in general) are always seen as THERE and THEN. This locus of behavior, the self, provides the context for all thoughts and emotions and enables or facilitates many different experiences, including theory of mind, empathy, compassion, self-compassion, acceptance, defusion, and a transcendent sense of self.

In the previous chapter, we described three modes of self that can be distinguished in the overall context of the self. One of these was *self-as-content*, which consists of elaborate self-descriptions built up over time. For example, "I am a thirty-year-old man; I am kind, slightly shy, witty...." Coherence in such stories is important because it facilitates a stable sense of self that allows one to predict and control his or her behavior, and for this reason people seek out evidence that confirms their self-narratives and discount evidence that does not fit. The downside of this is that people can easily become attached to or invested in particular experiences over others, and such a rigid, literal attachment to the conceptualized self can limit behavior. For instance, a rigid attachment to a concept of yourself as "shy" might make you less likely to socialize.

Attachment to mental content can, of course, be problematic in relationships, just as in other contexts. In a relationship, people have a story about the type of partner they are (self-as-content) and also a story about the type of person their partner is (other-as-content). Again, rigid attachment to these stories can be problematic.

As an example of attachment to mental content, imagine Karin, a young woman who has developed an attachment to a conceptualization of herself as having an attractive physical form. Karin is fit, weighing 121 pounds. She exercises regularly in order to maintain her figure. There is nothing wrong with keeping in shape, but for Karin, none of her physical activities are linked with a valued direction. If asked, Karin might say that she is terrified of gaining weight and becoming less attractive to potential dates. She weighs herself every day and only briefly feels good about herself—and even that is dependent on what the scale reveals. Karin's attachment to a concept of herself as having a perfect form makes for a highly structured existence that doesn't feel vital for very long. In addition, her physical form will inevitably change as she ages. Karin is likely to show up for therapy when she becomes exhausted or has been rejected in a relationship. In either of these cases, her conceptualized self will have been threatened.

Hence, attachment to self-as-content is potentially problematic, because it can cause people to lose contact with their values. The alternative to such problematic attachment is fostering a more all-inclusive and transcendent sense of the self: *self-as-context*.

ACT fosters this sense of self by teaching people to become more aware of their own psychological processes and to observe these processes with minimal evaluation. Both observation and non-evaluative description of private experiences can cultivate a sense of perspective to help people recognize that they are not defined, threatened, or controlled by their private experiences—that they can be aware of their flow of experiences without attachment to or investment in any particular experiences. Self-as-context is fostered in ACT to an important extent by the teaching of present awareness or mindfulness.

Present Awareness

Mindful awareness of what is happening moment-to-moment is necessary for responding adaptively and flexibly. People often get so caught up in their emotions, memories, bodily sensations, worries, and ruminations that they lose awareness of what is happening around them in the moment. Living "in their heads" and responding primarily to their own thoughts instead of what is actually going on is a key reason that people miss opportunities to live consistently with their values.

For example, Laura has a fear of losing her partner and has begun to obsess over thoughts of him leaving. She looks for signs of his displeasure with their relationship even as they talk together. In fact, she is sometimes so focused on these thoughts that she misses the substance of what he is saying. Her lack of attention to the present moment dulls the quality of their inter-actions. Her fearful thoughts put her on edge, and sometimes the couple end up arguing over small, irrelevant things. Laura is so enmeshed in her fear of losing her partner that she is, ironically, missing out on the enjoyment of her relationship and reducing the quality of the relationship for them both. In this way, her mindless fusion with fearful thoughts is undermining values-congruent behavior (i.e., committed action).

The alternative to getting caught up in mental content like this is to be mindfully aware of ongoing experiences, including self-as-process and other aspects. The more that people can do this, the better. To start with, people might need to get into the habit of deliberate mindfulness practice. A mindfulness session typically involves attending to physical sensations and thoughts and what is going on in one's environment, and attempting to simply experience these things without evaluating them. This promotes defused, nonjudgmental observation of experiences in general. It fosters an "observer" perspective that in turn enables people to see the "function" of their behavior.

From an RFT point of view, practicing mindfulness involves following a rule that prescribes attending to the immediately present experience. Doing so increases the behavior-regulatory effects of the experience and decreases typical levels of transformation of functions. People who practice mindfulness on an ongoing basis will likely increase their ability to discriminate aspects of their environment that may be important with respect to their valued goals (for example, their own and others' behavior in everyday social interactions). Ongoing practice will also facilitate the weakening of the behavior-regulatory effects of language, which is an important element of the ACT approach. With sufficient ongoing practice, the positive effects of present awareness may be discriminated and act to strengthen the operant, thus producing a positive feedback loop.

Mindfulness practice promotes an understanding of the transitory nature of psychological events and thus helps people simply accept those events as they are, instead of either avoiding them or clinging to them. In relationships, acceptance would imply being fully engaged with all related sensations, thoughts, and feelings without trying to change them. Unfortunately, fusion with verbal networks involving either positive or negative romantic experiences can remove people from the vitality and psychological flexibility of the present moment.

Let us consider negative thoughts and feelings first. RFT interprets these in terms of transformation of negative emotional functions through relational networks. Imagine that as you interact with a loved one, you think about losing this person and, as a result, experience fear and a feeling of loss. Such occasional feelings are the inevitable result of being a verbal human being. However, the context in which you experience those feelings is important. If the context is one of mindless fusion, you will likely derive further relations and may get caught up in a prolonged episode of negative thinking that will both be unpleasant and make you less sensitive to the contingencies of the present moment (e.g., the possibility of an intimate interaction with your loved one). However, if the context is one of mindful awareness, then you are more likely to be aware of the thought as just a thought and can continue to engage mindfully with your loved one. In the case of transformation of positive emotional functions, fusion can be pleasurable and relatively harmless in the short term, but the long-term consequences of a habit of thinking about, say, a relationship in romantic terms can have some of the same negative effects as fusion with negative events—namely, you become less sensitive to the environmental contingencies of the present moment. For example, the feeling of "being in love" includes transformation of functions through relational networks involving romantic images and stories. Fusion with these stories removes people from the experience of the present moment just as much as fusion with negative thoughts; ultimately, the pleasure derived from the story is transitory and artificial and can decrease the amount of real-life pleasure that may be had by being with the other person just as he or she is.

Both avoiding feelings that they don't want and indulging in romantic dreams can take people away from the reality of the present. It is only in the present moment that people can examine their sensations, thoughts, and feelings. ACT stresses the importance of willingness to be present to experiences, including especially aversive private experiences. Willingness provides an attitudinal foundation of acceptance, which helps people examine sensations and thoughts and gives them the opportunity to see these things for the transitory events they are, rather than the permanent entities they might sometimes appear to be. Willingness to stay with such private events enables people to pursue valued activities in relationships. People can learn to openly love and be loved while knowing that the feelings involved are temporary and that they should stay open to all feelings rather than cling to or avoid particular ones.

From what we have said above, it should be obvious how present awareness can facilitate self-as-context. Essentially, self-as-context can be thought of as the container for all of one's experiences, and present awareness allows one to come in contact with any and all of his or her experiences; thus, self-as-context is fostered in ACT to an important extent by the teaching of present awareness. These two intimately related processes then provide an important basis for the other two process pairs: mindful awareness of self-processes facilitates defusion from and acceptance of negative mental content, and both values and committed action are more likely from the perspective of a mindful, transcendent sense of self.

Relationships and Psychological Flexibility

Thus far we have examined several key processes that ACT sees as important in human psychology and have provided examples of how these processes can affect people, especially in the context of relationships. We have examined these processes in pairs because, as explained, certain pairs seem particularly complementary. However, ultimately, each of the processes described supports each of the others, and all target psychological flexibility—the process of contacting the present moment fully as a conscious human being and persisting in or changing certain behaviors in the service of chosen values. The goal of ACT work is to build psychological flexibility, which is characterized by broad repertoires of behavior that comport with valued directions.

One important aim of this chapter, of course, was to introduce ACT processes in the context of love and human relationships. For most people, establishing and maintaining a long-term intimate relationship is, indeed, a delicate and complex undertaking. And for some, intimate relationships may in fact present the greatest challenge in life. Love and intimacy create a context for the full spectrum of emotion, from euphoric highs to the depths of sorrow, in which emotions can change from one minute to the next. It is here, in the context of intimate relationships, that people's best and worst behavior patterns are revealed. Thus, intimate relationships represent an area of life in which people need psychological flexibility. They need to be open and make themselves vulnerable in order to establish an intimate relationship. They need to be in the present moment in order to find acceptance for all the feelings, physical sensations, and thoughts that bombard them. They need to keep the wisdom that all feelings come and go and that they have no control over feelings, thoughts, and physical sensations in order to refrain from chasing people they like or attempting to avoid people they don't. They need to be able to observe their thoughts as thoughts, even while they are occupied with verbal expectations, pictures, and ideals of how love should be, in order to make maximum contact with the reinforcing qualities of their relationship as it actually is. They need to be able to act in a loving manner, even when they don't feel loving, in order to stay true to the valued direction of intimacy. They need to nurture and maintain the balance of different life dimensions such as friends, health, and personal time in the presence of obsessive thoughts and feelings, in order to maximize the possibilities that life has to offer. Any intimate relationship is guaranteed to generate emotional challenges as well as emotional highs. Psychological flexibility can help people pass the difficult threshold of experiential avoidance and develop and maintain intimacy.

Summary

In this chapter, we introduced acceptance and commitment therapy (ACT), an approach to psychological functioning that coheres with the RFT conception of human language and suggests how human functioning might be optimized in accordance with this conception. We discussed the six ACT processes by examining the three complementary process pairs of acceptance and defusion, values and committed action, and self-as-context and present awareness; and, as we discussed each process, we considered examples of its relevance in the area of intimate relationships. Acceptance and defusion are needed to deal with the avoidance and fusion engendered by the sometimes aversive emotional experiences involved in a relationship. Values and committed action pertain to what is important about relationships and the actions needed to maintain them. The self is the context in which people experience all aspects of relationships, both positive and negative, while present awareness brings them into the fullest possible contact with all of these aspects. We concluded with a consideration of the overall ACT goal of psychological flexibility and the relevance of this goal for relationships. The nature of relationships is such that people who are in them can experience both extreme highs and extreme lows; as such, flexibility is particularly important.

CHAPTER 5

Language Traps and Self-as-Content

Introduction

Human love and sexuality is far richer and more complex than what is seen in other animals, due to the uniquely human verbal layer of behavior. Humans don't interact with sexual partners or potential partners merely at a physical or non-arbitrary level, as other animals do. Human beings also interact with their partner on a verbal level.

Once children become proficient at relational framing, they interact with their environment verbally and are influenced by it. This environment includes other people's nonverbal and verbal behavior and also, very importantly, includes one's own behavior. Self-produced rules can influence people in profound ways.

People who share a romantic relationship are constantly interacting verbally, not only with each other but also with their own separate learning histories, including rules and images related to ideals—the way things "should be"—of which they may not even be aware. In other words, each individual is constantly interacting with his or her own psychological content as well as that of his or her partner. All the processes of establishing and maintaining intimacy will be affected by this complex verbal layer of responding.

"The person who has been made aware of himself is in a better position to predict and control his own behavior" (Skinner, 1974, p. 35), and this verbal self-knowledge is essential for intimate relationships. For example, if you are in a new romantic relationship and you know that you tend to feel scared as a relationship becomes more serious, then you can be on the lookout for such fear and know that it likely signifies greater intimacy, as opposed to a serious problem.

At the same time, verbal self-awareness is the cause of human suffering, because verbal reports (i.e., thoughts and stories) of past painful events can elicit pain in the present. Remembering a traumatic breakup is likely to provoke feelings of anger, sadness, and fear, whether one is on the beach, sitting at home, or riding the subway. While people might naturally want to "not think" about painful events in their past in order to avoid such feelings in the present, such avoidance can be problematic and can sabotage intimate relationships.

In this chapter, we aim at illustrating how this verbal layer of responding may cause trouble in every phase of establishing and maintaining intimate relationships. We focus on the concept of "self-as-content" as a particularly hazardous perspective. Self-as-content involves relatively elaborate and well-rehearsed verbal self-descriptions and descriptions of one's behavior. These descriptions need not cohere well with current experience and indeed may be rigid and inflexible to such an extent that they interfere with contact with the current environment.

The ACT answer to self-as-content problems involves the cultivation of present awareness (mindfulness) and self-as-context. As the constant locus for behavior, self-as-context is all-inclusive and transcendent. As such, it can allow perspective on otherwise potentially problematic mental content and thus defuse it. As we explained in the last chapter, ACT fosters this sense of self by teaching people to become more aware of their own psychological processes and to observe these processes with minimal evaluation. This involves teaching mindful awareness of ongoing external events, including self-as-process (i.e., ongoing events happen *to* one). In relationships, one other class of events of which it is important to be mindfully aware is other-as-process, in which ongoing events happen to another person. Mindful awareness of both self-as-process and other-as-process (see chapter 3) can enrich people's experiences, particularly intimate interactions with their partner.

Early in a relationship, lovers may respond in a relatively mindful way. The novelty of the experience might help each person be open to learning about the other. Over time, however, one or both partners may start reacting increasingly frequently to psychological content, which is elaborated and removed (i.e., self-as-content) rather than current. The partners might start accumulating thoughts, memories, and feelings about each other and the relationship, which increases the likelihood of problematic verbal responding.

Confusion, and likely problems, arise when elaborated psychological content is presented and reacted to as if it were current. For example, intimate touching may elicit both sensual pleasure, which is current (self-as-process), and aversive memories of feeling extreme guilt about intimate touching (self-as-content). If one reacts to self-as-content as if it were self-as-process, he or she might act to avoid intimate touching despite the potential pleasure. In this way, the aversive functions of the verbal construction override the potential reinforcers of the present situation and trigger avoidance. What could and should be pleasurable and enriching for the partnership becomes instead aversive and problematic.

In this chapter, we present the general concept of self-as-content as it is defined in ACT and RFT. Self-as-content is broken down into a number of aspects that can be particularly problematic in intimate relationships. These "language traps," in turn, are based on different forms of verbal fusion. Fusion with psychological content is often expressed in terms of life roles, rules, stereotypes, feelings, and evaluations of feelings. Identifying with such simplifications and stereotypes of themselves, their partner, and the nature of "love" can pull people away from potentially life-enriching intimate experiences.

Fusion with Self-as-Content

This is how the self-as-content platform is usually built: At about the age of four, children develop a concept of distinguishable self, and around puberty they start using self-descriptions of psychological characteristics, including competencies, emotions, values, and traits (Damon & Hart, 1988). Schools, society, and family dictate how this self should develop and prompt comparison with others. Competition and achievement of specific goals determines the success of this self.

At some point, there is a gap between the self one perceives and the expectation of who he or she should be. Continued comparisons with others (e.g., how one looks, how one acts, what one achieves, or what one owns compared to others) will, over time, lead to the derivation that one is less than others in at least some respects. This contributes to a concept and accompanying feeling of self-deficiency.

Gilbert (2007) and others have provided evidence of the "deficient self" by showing that, in many important respects, people have a lifelong negative bias when comparing themselves to others. The discomfort of this "deficient self" shows up in social situations, especially those in which one is subject to scrutiny, such as when speaking in public. In these situations, people likely judge that there is a high risk that their deficient self will be revealed. Attempts to hide the deficient self and avoid the discomfort of its revelation could result in several categories of experiential avoidance: the use of substances like alcohol and drugs, or food; or behaviors, like excessive sex, shopping, or exercise.

Of particular relevance in the current context is that the "deficient self" may set the stage for experiential avoidance in relationships. Establishing intimate relationships requires phys-ical and verbal closeness and openness. However, fears that the deficient self will be revealed are especially likely under these circumstances. These fears will likely trigger avoidant behavior patterns that will preclude full enjoyment of the relationship. For example, fighting, judging one's partner, or blaming one's partner for feelings of deficiency can constitute a category of avoidant behavior. Attempting to please one's partner or conform to his or her wishes ("compensatory pliance") consti-tutes another. In both of these cases, an unhealthy pattern of interaction is set up in order to avoid the deficient self, and the result is less contact with the reinforcement that the relation-ship has to offer.

From an ACT/RFT point of view, the "deficient self" is a product of fusion with self-as-content. Self-as-content is a par-ticular perspective on the world in which the world is struc-tured by the literal meaning of one's psychological content. Here are some examples.

"I am sad."

"I am a good person."

"I am angry at you."

"I am fat and unattractive."

"I am unlovable."

"I don't trust people."

In these examples, it is quite likely that the speaker is fused with, or believes fully in, the literal truth of the statement—its psychological content. A rigid adherence to content of the mind such as this (i.e., one's verbal relational repertoire), is potentially problematic. For example, believing in the literal truth of such negative self-evaluations as "I am unattractive" can feel pretty hopeless.

To take an example from the list above, reacting to "I am fat and unattractive" as a verbal truth would likely make it difficult to establish intimacy in a relationship. This is because establishing intimacy means letting your partner see you as you are; however, if you are convinced you are unattractive, you are likely to try to avoid being seen in this way. To take another example, responding to "I don't trust people" as a fact would make trusting behavior less likely. Fusion creates an apparently irresolvable dilemma in this case, because the cause of the distrust is in the past, and the past cannot be changed. Reacting to this mental content as if it were true *here and now* functions as a guide to future behavior and is likely to restrict opportunities for intimate interaction. Put another way, fusion with such thoughts makes them into obstacles to taking steps in the direction of such values as intimacy.

Self-as-content consists of elaborate descriptive and evaluative relational networks that people, over time, construct about themselves and their individual history. As indicated above, as soon as children become self-aware, they begin to create a "self" by organizing particular descriptions, evaluations, histories, and tendencies into a fairly consistent presentation. Perhaps for the rest of their lives, they will seek coherence in this sense of self. Interpretation, explanation, evaluation, prediction, and rationalization are examples of attempts to achieve this coherence. For instance, consider the following statements:

"I've never been very good at expressing my feelings."

"As the child of an alcoholic, I have trust issues."

"I know how this relationship will end, so what is the use of trying?"

In each of these examples, the speaker has constructed a story about his or her self in order to achieve coherence. The person who is fused with the story "I've never been very good at expressing my feelings" may be rationalizing poor attempts to express feelings. In the second example, the person attributes a lack of trusting behavior to a past event. The third example illustrates rationalization of avoidance of attempts to establish intimacy based on an implicit rule that the past reliably predicts the future.

In all of these examples, the speaker is fused with historical psychological content and sees his or her current reality, including potential relationships, through the lens of this created self. Fusion with this constructed self would definitely put a damper on the potential for experiencing richly intimate moments in relationships. This type of self-evaluation not only describes past behavior but actually guides future behavior. In addition, at the heart of these examples is experiential avoidance— because the discomfort involved in showing feelings, putting trust in another, or engaging in relationships in the knowledge that they are temporary is avoided. The speakers gain short-term relief from the anxiety of the situation, but they do so at the expense of their quality of life in the long run. The alternative would be to take steps toward intimacy, a valued direction, and accept or make room for the inevitable discomfort.

In order to maintain coherence in their self-stories, people will strive to act in accordance with those stories. In fact, they may even ignore contradictory evidence and actually select only that which is consistent with their self-story. Consider the following example.

Yolanda is fused with the story that historically she has not been seen, validated, and loved in a way that she deserves. She also believes that her current partner does not see, validate, and love her the way she expects. She has mentally compiled a list of evidence showing that her partner doesn't love her. The theme she expresses is an old, familiar one: "After all I have done in this relationship, I deserve better." Each time Yolanda ruminates on this theme in one of many variations, she cries and feels sorry for herself. From an outsider's perspective, this behavior may look peculiar, because her partner does seem to love and care for her and often does things that appear to show this. However, Yolanda disregards her partner's expressions of love and caring and selects events that support her self-story. By striving to maintain her story, Yolanda is destroying her relationship. Rather than reinforcing her partner's efforts to show love, she is punishing them. Although Yolanda values her relationship and wants to act in a loving way toward her partner, fusion with the story "My partner doesn't love me" triggers reactions and responses that are the opposite of loving behavior and, in fact, function as punishment for loving behavior, both for herself and for her partner. It creates a feedback loop and keeps loving behavior away.

Self-as-content may include fusion with psychological content from a variety of domains of experience as well as with historical feelings, sensations, and preferences, and all of this psychological content may then become mixed up with what is happening *here and now*. Whenever people express their likes or dislikes with regard to intimate interactions, it is most likely from the perspective of self-as-content. Such fusion with ideas or stereotypes regarding oneself or a potential partner is not necessarily problematic; however, it will inevitably limit

111

opportunities for intimate experiences. One arena in which this is apparent is online dating. Dating sites are built on self-as-content. When creating an online dating profile, users are asked to characterize or stereotype themselves as well as to identify their preferences in a partner. This task requires a self-as-content perspective, because users must provide a verbal elaboration or summary of themselves. Dating sites are useful in that they provide an opportunity to meet potential partners; however, users should understand that the categories and checklists these sites provide are not literal truths about potential partners.

Suppose that Sue decides to try online dating. She creates her profile, characterizing herself in terms of age, education level, weight, sexual orientation, religion, ethnic origin, and preferences as far as food, music, and leisure activities. She fills in a similar list with regard to her preferences for a potential partner. Again, many of these preferences may be built on historical experience. It might be safe to say that some of her preferences (for example, to find someone who enjoys the same kind of food or music) are likely to be based more on prejudices, wishes, stereotypes, and dreams than on actual experience.

If, in the context of dating, people are fused with mental content in the form of preferences and stereotypes regarding potential partners, then that content will tend to exert control over their dating behavior. Even if people value being open-minded and experiential, they are likely to close down when fused with this "story" of their preferences. Ideally, those who want to find a partner will be helped by being in the "here and now" while relating to their preferences in a flexible manner. This implies understanding and relating to mental content as content, not as who one is or who others are.

Suppose that according to the dating site's analysis, Andy is a very good match with Sue's wish list of criteria. After they speak on the telephone, Sue arranges to meet Andy at a cafe. The two have seen each other's pictures, and both have strong expectations based on the other's online profile. At that meeting are not just Sue and Andy, but also their minds, which are constantly evaluating and judging the other person according to these mental constructs. Rather than a meeting between Sue and Andy, it is a meeting between Sue's self-as-content and Andy's self-as-content. As not infrequently happens, both Sue and Andy walk away disappointed; even though each's self-as-content made for a good match, they felt no attraction. This is because when self-as-content dominates, present-moment experimentation takes a backseat and an intimate connection is less likely. The more mindful two people are when they meet, however, the more likely there will be a meaningful exchange, even if it turns out that they aren't fated to become a couple.

Mental Content as the "Cause" of Behavior

Self-as-content can sometimes be perceived as a cause of—and, thus, either implicitly or explicitly, become an excuse for—current maladaptive patterns of behavior. This is the "content as cause" language trap. Here are some examples of this particular language trap as it might operate in an intimate relationship:

> "I can't be open with you because I never learned to trust people."

113

"I don't feel comfortable with your family because they're different from what I'm used to."

"I won't commit to a same-sex partner because I was taught that such relationships are wrong and can never last."

In each of these examples, the speaker is explaining why he or she is not acting in a caring, loving, open way by using psychological content from the past as the "cause." With this line of reasoning, the only way to change the present (and thus begin to act in a trusting, open manner) would be to change the past. In the first example, for the speaker to be open and trusting, he or she would need to have learned how to do that in the past. In the second example, for the speaker to act in an open and accepting manner with the new family, he or she would have had to experience a similar family in the past. Since that is not possible, the "excuse" not to behave in this valued direction hampers the development of intimacy. Fusion with these thoughts can create a feedback loop in which this individual may feel as if he or she has lost the ability to change his or her behavior and take steps in a valued direction. Partners can know and agree on valued directions in their relationships, as well as what behaviors would coincide with those values, but fusion with psychological content may sabotage those attempts. Such fusion creates the illusion that the future is determined by the past. However, while past behavior can certainly allow prediction of future behavior, it does not determine it.

Another similar language trap stems from relying on verbal reasons as causes of behavior. People have a tendency to seek to explain why they do things and why they do not have the things in their lives that they want. They learn early in life that the "whys" can be linked to a cause, and if there is a cause, then they may be able to predict and possibly even control the effects of this cause. In many areas of life, this is a useful strategy, but when it comes to feelings and behavior in intimate relationships, looking for reasons can get people off track. In identifying instances of this language trap, it may be useful to look for statements that have an if-then causal relationship, along the lines of "If my partner would just change his behavior, then I could act more the way I want to act." Following are some examples:

"If my partner would show me a little more love and attention when we go out, I would be in a better mood."

"If only my partner would show more interest in sex, I would feel more attractive."

"If only my partner would take more responsibility for the kids, I could go back to school and do something with my life."

The problem here is that there are actually very few true "cause and effect" relationships in the realm of interpersonal behavior. Such statements as those just listed create the illusion of a simple "cause and effect" relationship; however, it is typically not the case that when some first condition is fulfilled some other condition will directly result. If people think that their bad mood, not feeling attractive, or not going back to school is being "caused" by their partner's behavior, they might predict that a change in their partner's behavior will solve the problem. In reality, however, many other factors figure into the situation. Given the complex relationships between events, people are generally not very good at describing the "if" part of such statements accurately, and are never assured of the "then" part.

Fusion with these statements of simple cause-and-effect relations can lock people into an excuse for stagnation. However, the speakers in all the examples above *could* act in the way they wanted, regardless of whether their partner changed his or her behavior. The first could influence his or her own mood swings; the second could help himself or herself feel attractive; and the third could decide to go back to school anyway.

In addition, problems arise in relationships when the conditions set forth in the "if" part of the statement are not likely to be fulfilled. If the partner with the supposedly limiting behavior is unlikely to ever change, this effectively keeps the other partner far from the "then" part of the statement.

Fusion with Life Roles

Another variety of language trap that can operate in an intimate relationship is based on fusion with a particular role that one sees oneself having in that relationship.

Everyone develops roles in a relationship. Roles can refer to household responsibilities, like "the one who cooks," "the one who drives the car," "the one who disciplines the children," or "the one who likes having friends over." Role divisions like this may be functional and help the household run smoothly and predictably. However, when taken literally, they may hem people in and lead to feelings of restriction, constraint, and stagnation. Roles are always an oversimplification; people are complex and ever-changing.

Roles may also refer to psychological (often stereotypical) functions: "the loving housewife," "the jealous husband," "the controlling wife," "the aggressive (or passive) partner," "the overbearing or unfaithful husband," and so forth. Such unidimensionality is characteristic of lesser-quality fiction. While strictly delineating the "good guys" from the "bad guys" and having characters behave in predictable ways may make a novel easier to read, it might be said that more literary novels more accurately reflect human complexity. For example, Dostoyevsky's characters change and evolve over time, making them far more exciting and unpredictable than flat or static ones. In the same way as a less gifted writer might, people may stereotype themselves and their partners in terms of psychological content. Casting a partner as the "shy one," "the one who wants less sex," or "the control freak" is likely to maintain this very behavior. Repeating these role stereotypes either to oneself or to one's partner actually increases the likelihood of behavior that conforms to them.

Some roles are based on cultural ideals. In Western society the "good" husband, the "benevolent" wife, and the "nuclear" family are examples of roles for which people are programmed. In collectivist cultures, a family consisting only of a mother, a father, and their children is less likely to be seen as an ideal than it is in individualist cultures, such as ours. Yet in Europe and most of North America, the nuclear family is still the ideal, despite evidence that families are actually quite diverse: in many families, there is only one parent; in others, multiple generations live together; in some, children are raised by grandparents; and, in others, children are raised by two parents of the same gender. In fact, the 1950s American ideal of Dad working in a great job to pay for the home in the suburbs, Mom at home baking pies, and two lovely children (a boy and a girl, of course) is far from reality for most—or, as Coontz (1992) states, "the way we never were." Yet, some form of an absolute ideal exists in all societies and provides idealized roles that may keep people from experiencing life as it is in contemporary society. People who accept their own and others' families as they actually are, in all of their variety, rather than trying to distort themselves or expecting others to do so in order to follow an ideal, are better able to live *here and now.*

While certain aspects of idealized roles may be functional, roles are always liable to pull people away from experiential and ongoing presence with the "here and now." The feeling of responsibility to fill a role may trump the feelings that arise in the present moment. For example, though a woman in the role of the loving housewife may actually feel suffocated and long to experiment in the working world, she may disregard her own feelings in service of this role; the discrepancy between how she actually feels (suffocated) and how she is supposed to feel in this role (happy) can lead her to think that there is something wrong with how she is feeling. Lesbians and gay men who follow societal, familial, or personal pressures to marry someone of the opposite sex find themselves emotionally and sexually unfulfilled (as do their spouses). In these situations, alcohol, tranquilizers, or extramarital lovers might serve as distractions from those feelings.

Stereotypes don't just apply to individuals; they can also apply to couples. This happens when the couple is regarded as a unit. Stereotyping might involve socioeconomic status (e.g., the middle-class couple), education level (e.g., the academic couple), or sexual orientation (e.g., the gay couple). Any category used elicits associations and evaluations of those associations, both from the couple and from others. In the same way, fusion with these roles as a couple can reduce sensitivity to inevitable changes and make adapting to meet these changes difficult.

Fusion with Rules

In a previous chapter, we provided an RFT explanation of rules as networks of verbal relations that influence people's behavior by transforming the functions of their environment through these relations.

Rules can be helpful. Skinner (1989) contrasted rule-governed behavior with contingency-shaped behavior by pointing out that while nonhuman animals often have to learn how to adapt to their environment by means of trial and error, humans can adapt quickly by following rules specifying how to behave in particular situations. Rules can guide people to act in ways that others before them have found useful. A recipe, for instance, consists of a set of rules originally created by someone who, through experimentation, found a useful way to cook a dish. Following this set of rules saves other people the time and effort of experimenting and, hopefully, leads to a tasty result.

In sexual relationships, rules regarding preferences of intimate interaction can be helpful. For example, one partner might say "I like it when I come home from work and you give me a back rub." This rule specifies spatial and temporal antecedents, the topography of the response, and the nature of the consequence. The other partner can hear this rule once and act in accordance with it without any other input. Rules like these save partners from having to figure out each other's preferences through trial and error.

However, rules can also be unhelpful. In the ACT tradition, the focus is typically on informal rules that people derive about their personal situation that affect them negatively. For example, after a number of rejections from women he meets online, Jeff derives the rule "No one will ever want to be with me," which

119

subsequently guides his behavior away from dating in general, despite the fact that dating is consistent with his valued direction. In other words, Jeff takes the rule he has derived literally and gives up.

What makes such rules as Jeff's particularly unhelpful is that they remove people from direct contact with contingencies. There is much empirical research showing the phenomenon of rule-based insensitivity to contingencies, whereby people under the influence of rules are much less likely to adapt to changes in their environment (e.g., Hayes, Brownstein, Haas, & Greenway, 1986; Matthews, Shimoff, Catania, & Sagvolden, 1977; Shimoff, Catania, & Matthews, 1981). In the example just given, Jeff comes under the influence of his self-generated rule and stops dating. However, when he stops dating, he is cut off from the contingency whereby dating can allow him to meet someone compatible. In other words, he no longer has the chance of meeting someone with whom he might enjoy himself and establish a successful relationship. The rule has cut him off from this possibility. If Jeff were able to see this rule as a mere thought among other thoughts, he would probably persist in dating and would at least have a chance of contacting the reinforcement of acceptance and intimacy when someone suitable came along. However, by fusing with his self-generated rule, he stops trying, and this possibility is ruled out.

Following unhelpful rules can also cut people off from contingencies within an already established relationship. Sensitivity is essential in establishing and maintaining intimate relationships. However, rule-following can reduce sensitivity to cues in the present moment, and when this happens in a relationship, partners are likely to get off the intimate track. For example, George invites Frank to move into his apartment after a passionate year-long relationship. However, in this new context, differences between the two become apparent. George is very particular about neatness and order. He has derived the general rule that someone who is not neat is being inconsiderate. Frank, while not slovenly, is much more laid-back in this respect. After they move in together, Frank's patterns of laid-back behavior quickly become apparent to George, who derives that Frank is being inconsiderate to him. Frank notes George's displeasure and tries to make his behavior conform a bit more to what he thinks George wants. However, his old habits are strong and he sometimes forgets. The arguments that break out gradually escalate. One day, in a huge fight, George tells Frank that he no longer sees in him the person whom he wanted to be with forever; instead, he sees someone who is taking advantage of his generosity. Frank decides that he has had enough and moves out.

George's fusion with his own rule-based interpretation of the way things should be overrides his sensitivity to the fact that Frank has a different history and a different attitude. There is little room for negotiation of the inevitable changes that take place once two people move in together. More importantly, George's rule-following overrides his sensitivity to Frank's attempts to conform to his requests, as well as his ability to notice the things he loves about Frank. George's fusion with rule-following about neatness comes at the expense of his valued direction of developing intimacy, and costs him his relationship.

Thus, rules can be very influential, all too often in a negative way, as the example above illustrates. Chapter 3 referred to a number of different categories of rules based on the three different kinds of contingencies that produce rule-following behavior: pliance, tracking, and augmenting. It is helpful to call these categories to mind in the current context, because they can provide additional insight when examining how partners relate to rules regarding intimate interactions.

Pliance is rule-governed behavior under the influence of a history of socially mediated reinforcement for following rules. This means that an individual follows a rule simply because he or she has been reinforced in the past for rule-following. Here are some examples of what pliance might look like in an intimate relationship.

Doing something in order to please one's partner

Doing something in order to avoid conflicts or outbursts

Doing something in order to look good in the eyes of others

In each of these examples, the function or intention of the response is to please others or avoid punishment from them. Pliance is the category of rule-governed behavior that is most associated with psychopathology, because the rule-following is done in the service of an unstable source of reinforcement (i.e., the approval of other people) irrespective of the environmental contingencies, and thus this category of rule-following in particular focuses on the rule rather than on the contingencies. As we have said before, establishing and maintaining intimacy requires sensitivity to the "here and now"—the natural environmental contingencies. Pliance, however, encourages greater sensitivity to the rules, at the expense of contact with what's actually happening in the present moment.

Example:

Natural contingencies (sensitive to cues in present moment)
"I feel aroused when you touch me right now."

Pliance

"My plan for us tonight is dinner, a movie, and then sex."

In the first statement, the speaker is in contact with sensations resulting from intimate touch and is verbalizing a liking for it, which helps guide the listener toward greater intimacy. In the second statement, in contrast, the speaker is verbalizing a rule or agenda that appears to be independent of the natural contingencies of what's unfolding in real time—that is, what both partners are feeling or desiring in the moment. Such an agenda might be considered pliance, because it suggests sex for reasons of social conformity (i.e., "We should have sex regularly because that's what people do"). If, to please or placate the speaker, the listener engages in sex as part of the speaker's plan, then that is of course also pliance.

Tracking is a form of rule-governed behavior under the control of a history of coordination between a rule and the arrangement of the environment independently of the rule's delivery.

Tracking in an intimate relationship might be similar to what some call trying to "read" a partner's behavior, likes, and dislikes. Tracking the other person's behavior patterns could help the tracker know how to adapt his or her behavior. This might include constructing an ongoing verbal "other-as-process" through the use of questions (e.g., "What are you thinking?" "Do you like when I do that?") and then responding sensitively based on the answers.

Tracking in a relationship thus requires the ability to take one's partner's perspective to an important extent, and this ability seems to be an essential skill in building intimacy. Conversely, problems with tracking occur when the tracker is interpreting and evaluating the partner's behavior based on his or her own psychological content (e.g., memories of another partner or worries about sexual performance) rather than on the interaction *here and now*.

Augmenting is rule-governed behavior that alters the degree to which events function as consequences. Motivative augmenting, for example, changes the effectiveness of a stimulus already functioning as a consequence. If, for example, your partner calls you in your car and says, "I have a wonderful dinner waiting for you when you get home," this is likely to increase the reinforcing effect of your dinner. Self-rules can be value statements, like "I would like more intimacy with my partner." This kind of rule might function to increase the likelihood of behaviors that move one in the direction of this value and punish behaviors that move one away from it. For example, opportunities to get more time alone with your partner might be made more reinforcing, while activities that reduce time with your partner might become more punishing.

Augmenting can be problematic when behaviors that are antithetical to a healthy partnership are encouraged. For example, some groups (e.g., political conservatives) may promote the rule (sometimes implicitly and sometimes explicitly) that women should stay at home to care for children. This cultural value might motivate dominance in some men ("the breadwinner") and subservience in some women ("the housewife"), thus arguably undermining the possibility of relationships in which both partners are truly equal participants. Following rules related to such stereotyped gender roles can be inhibiting and stressful for both partners when these group norms do not represent their freely chosen values.

Fusion with Thoughts About Feelings: Emotional Language

Feelings and emotions are obviously an important aspect of romantic relationships. They can sometimes be very positive, and they can sometimes be very negative. From an ACT perspective, the extent and nature of the influence of emotions can be problematic whether they are positive or negative. Fusion with thoughts about feelings represents another potential language trap, and the way in which people come to think and talk about their emotions as a result of conventional emotional training by the verbal community can be troublesome. Let us examine the various qualities of conventional emotional training.

First, emotional language is inexact. The verbal community teaches people to discriminate and describe how they feel in the same way it teaches them to describe external objects, such as a pen or a cat. However, there is an important difference. External objects are publicly observable. Feelings are only partially observable; they are indirectly observable through behaviors that are *possible* indications of the feelings in question but are never directly the feelings themselves. A parent or caregiver might say to a child who is crying, "You feel sad." However, this verbal label of a presumed feeling is, of course, much less precise than saying "This is a cat" in the presence of a cat. This is because the parent or caregiver really has no direct concept of how the child is feeling. He or she is simply reacting to what he or she thinks the child is feeling. Thus, training discrimination of emotional states is less precise than might be desired.

Another problematic aspect of people's emotional training is that they are taught to see emotions as important

125

determinants of behavior. For instance, they learn that saying things like "I felt like (or didn't feel like) doing X" is typically accepted as a valid reason for doing or not doing X, whatever X might be (going to a party, attending a job interview, getting up, etc.), even though in actuality there is no necessary connection between feelings and behavior—in other words, one could do X or not do X whatever one's feelings. This type of training teaches people to see feelings and emotions as potentially important determiners of their lives at a psychological level, and when they are fused with this idea they will very likely act accordingly.

Add to these features the fact that the verbal community also teaches people to evaluate their experiences as good or bad. If a child's caregivers evaluate a certain feeling as "sad" or as "bad," then the child is likely to learn to evaluate feelings in this way also. Once the child learns this dichotomy of "good" versus "bad" feelings and begins to fuse with these evaluations, he or she will likely start trying to avoid bad feelings and to seek out good ones. From the perspective of self-as-content, good and bad feelings come to be taken literally, as if they were places that one might actually reach or, alternatively, avoid.

These aspects of people's emotional training are potentially problematic in all domains of life, but perhaps not least in the context of intimate relationships.

A learned inexactitude with respect to emotions is relevant in an intimate relationship, because expressing feelings or using emotional language is often prioritized in relationships. In the course of establishing a romantic relationship, people typically use phrases like "I love you" and "I feel love for you." People are taught that they are discriminating a feeling when they say "I love you," but what exactly that feeling is or how intense it needs to be to occasion those words is subjective. For this reason and other reasons of personal history, what such terms as "love," "desire," "care," and "adore" actually mean in emotional language may differ between partners. Such differences may be a source of conflict. For example, one partner might associate sexual exclusivity with the expression "I love you," while the other partner might not.

Seeing emotions as behavioral determinants is problematic in general, because feelings are relatively unstable—they change over time. Relationships, in particular, involve highs and lows. Sometimes people can feel what seems like "true love," while at other times they might not be sure; after a big argument, people can feel anger and even hatred toward each other. In addition, passion often fades or changes over the years. Older couples may not feel the same depth or kind of emotion that younger couples do. Given such changes in emotion, both in the short term and in the long term, fusion with emotional thoughts—allowing emotion to dominate behavior—has the potential to make human relationships very unstable.

The tendency to evaluate emotions is also problematic. Emotions are neither good nor bad in an absolute sense but are mere sensations that come and go, changing all the time. When a private event is viewed as "good," there is a tendency to cling to it, and when a private event is evaluated as "bad," there is a tendency to avoid it. As we have just discussed, however, in intimate relationships in particular, emotions rise and fall all the time, and thus both clinging and avoidant behaviors will likely be counterproductive.

In summary, a number of aspects of learned emotional responding can be problematic in the area of intimate relationships. Emotions are subjective; they can change from one minute to the next; they can be relatively intense. And yet people are taught to regard them as determining influences on their behavior and to pursue good feelings and avoid bad ones, to the detriment of stable and psychologically healthy potential guides of behavior—such as values, for example.

This emotional training is both influential and problematic in intimate relationships, because intimate feelings are both powerful and subject to change. If relationship behavior is steered by as temporary as feelings, then the relationship will be unstable. Emotions are important, but people should not let themselves be dominated by them. ACT would suggest the importance of values rather than emotions as core determiners of behavior in relationships. In a later chapter (chapter 7), we contrast values-based behavior with feelings-based behavior in intimate relationships.

Summary

Language enriches the experience of love and intimacy, but it also creates problems. In this chapter, we focused on entanglement with language. Fusion with self-as-content is a potential danger in intimate interactions. Elaborating on this concept, we broke self-as-content down into a number of aspects that can be particularly problematic in intimate relationships. These different "language traps," in turn, are based on different forms of verbal fusion, including fusion with life roles, fusion with rules, and fusion with (thoughts about) emotions. ACT suggests that the alternative to fusion with self-as-content is mindful awareness, including self-as-process, which helps people defuse from language traps in order to act in accordance with their values. We return to this idea later on, when we examine the ACT prescription for healthy relationships. In the next chapter, we examine a second potentially problematic phenomenon within intimate relationships: psychological rigidity.

CHAPTER 6

Psychological Rigidity

Introduction

The evolved capacity to avoid or escape danger or aversive conditions is something that we humans share with many other species, and it is a capacity that has had tremendous survival value throughout our history. However, unlike other animals, due to the special properties of human language, we also attempt to prevent, avoid, and escape thoughts and feelings connected with (or, more specifically, relationally framed with) potentially dangerous situations. In relationships, this tendency to avoid aversive thoughts or feelings may trap people in patterns of behavior that are inconsistent with their values. As we have previously suggested, avoidance behavior under aversive control (i.e., responding to what might be referred to as "negative events") tends to be rigid, rule-bound, and less vital than behavior under appetitive control (i.e., responding to what might be referred to as "positive events"), which tends to be flexible, exploratory, and vital. In this chapter, we focus on what happens when responding in relationships is characterized by experiential avoidance and subsequently psychological rigidity.

Getting Stuck in Non-vital Patterns in Relationships

People get stuck in behavior that leads to non-vital relationships when avoidance trumps approach. *Psychological rigidity* is defined in ACT as maladaptive behavior that serves as avoidance of aversive stimuli. Rigidity is often characterized by suffering caused by negative thoughts, feelings, and memories that get in the way of vital living. Simply said, often people spend valuable time and energy trying to get rid of negative private events at the cost of actually living life and partaking of the joys present in the "here and now." In relationships, psychological rigidity sometimes traps people in impulsive, self-defeating actions or inactions that sabotage vitality in intimacy.

The Special Challenges of an Intimate Relationship

Because all relationships by definition involve two or more people who are different from each other in a variety of ways, they inevitably involve conflicts of interest and differing agendas that require some degree of adaptive social skills and psychological flexibility to navigate. Intimate relationships are not qualitatively different with regard to these challenges, but the emotions involved are likely to be more intense. One of the probable reasons for this is the high expectations that are due to, among other things, romantic myths in popular media and literature. These myths include the "perfect partner": someone who will complete you, with whom love will be easy, and with whom you'll live entirely happily after the wedding or commitment ceremony. People with these types of expectations of romantic love are in for special challenges. Before we examine the nature of those challenges in a bit more detail, it might be useful to first consider the nature of the romantic context in which they arise, by examining different levels or stages of intimacy.

Stages of Intimacy

Our discussion of stages of intimacy is based on Fisher's theory of emotional systems or emotional categories (Fisher, Aron, & Brown, 2005). In this approach, there are three qualitatively different categories, lust, romantic love, and attachment, each of which is underpinned by a different biochemical system. Fisher suggests that intimacy can start off with any of these three feelings. However, perhaps the most common ordering in the development of a romantic relationship would be lust, followed by romantic attraction, and then attachment. In what follows, we consider them in this order, as a theory of stages of the development of intimacy.

The first category or stage, lust, involves animal attraction—a motivation to have sex with any semi-compatible partner. This stage is associated with testosterone and estrogen in both men and women.

The second stage, romantic love, is characterized by behavior focused on one particular partner. This is commonly called infatuation or casually referred to as being "madly" in love. Fisher has shown that people who are "madly" in love produce greater quantities of dopamine, and this may explain the strength of the feelings and the consequent "madness" and irrationality that are involved: people love being in love. Apart from higher levels of dopamine, romantic love also increases levels of norepinephrine and serotonin. Feeling "in love" creates a sense of vitality as well as a sharp focus on the object of that love. In evolutionary terms, this type of romantic feeling helped our ancestors choose and pursue certain mating partners and then start the mating process. However, this stage of intimacy cannot maintain for long; according to Fisher, it lasts between six and eighteen months.

As the effect of the second-stage chemicals lessens, the third stage of intimacy starts. Attachment is characterized by a motivation toward "nesting," or wanting to live with a partner. This stage is based on the neurotransmitters oxytocin and vasopressin. It typically marks the beginning of a relatively long-term monogamous relationship whose purpose, from an evolutionary perspective, is procreation and the raising of children. Of course, many modern "long-term life partnerships" do not involve children; nevertheless, the raising of offspring is the likely evolutionary origin of this ultimate stage. Whether or not a couple choose to raise children, the defining characteristic of this phase is a long-term romantic relationship.

Each of the three categories or stages presents special challenges, but the majority of people who seek therapy for relationship difficulties are most likely to be in the third and final stage, attachment. During the second stage, romantic love, partners are likely to regulate each other's anxiety by validating each other frequently. For example, you give in to your partner on one issue, and he or she gives in to you on another. This keeps anxiety at bay, and both partners feel loved and validated. However, the compromises involved at this stage are not reached without some ambivalence, and usually at some point one partner doesn't want to adapt.

Partners who share a romantic history and have now chosen each other in a committed relationship often have difficulty sustaining vitality. Whereas during the romantic love stage, it is quite easy to agree to disagree about abstract things—such as emotions, political ideas, perceptions, or values—once two people choose to live together and interact daily, their differences more directly affect them. The most common areas of confrontation brought to therapy are similar in all types of relationships and include sexual wants and needs, ways of handling money, ways of bringing up children, and frequency of interaction with extended family (e.g., Kurdek, 2004). How a couple handle these conflicts may predict how the relationship grows and develops. If one or both partners develop patterns of avoidance of conflict itself, this will likely lead to stagnation and less vitality in the relationship. Patterns of avoidance and/or rigidity within conflict can also be problematic.

Psychological Rigidity in Relationship Conflicts

As human beings, we all try to control what happens to us both internally and externally. We tend to want to experience only "positive" emotions, and we get stressed, angry, or disappointed when things are not the way we wish them to be. In relationships, we strive to carve out a personal space in coexistence with a partner who is also striving for personal space. In this space, we attempt to balance our own needs, desires, and interests with those of the other person. Obviously this work must involve compromise and adaptation.

Conflict, far from being antithetical, is an important source of growth in an intimate relationship. Confrontation tests a couple's ability to solve problems while staying on a valued track. In order to strengthen rather than weaken their relationship, however, partners need to be mindful of the rigid, self-defeating behavior patterns that often arise during conflicts. In other words, the way in which people deal with conflicts—and in particular the level of rigidity or flexibility that they bring to them—shapes their relationships and to a great degree determines the level of vitality therein. For some examples of psychological responding in the context of relationship conflict, let's consider one possible source of conflict: how frequently each partner wants sex.

Differences in Sexual Desire

Schnarch (2011) suggests that a common reason couples seek therapy is that one partner wants sex more often than the other.

He proposes that in nearly all couples there is a consistent high-desire role and a consistent low-desire role. The high-desire partner, who wants more sex, will naturally be rejected on a regular basis. Rejection may elicit thoughts of not being good enough, with accompanying transformations of negative emotional stimulus functions, experienced as feelings of discomfort and insecurity. How this partner deals with these thoughts and feelings will be critical to the development of the relationship.

Here is one possible scenario. Jemima approaches Imran with a seductive kiss suggesting that she would like to engage in sexual activity. Imran responds that he is tired and would like to rest. Jemima feels hurt, rejected, and unattractive. As she has done on many evenings previously, she pours herself a large glass of wine to numb this feeling. Jemima's drinking makes her even less attractive in Imran's eyes and makes any sexual activity even less likely that evening.

Jemima's intolerance of her own discomfort elicits avoidant behavior that pulls her and Imran further away from intimacy and in a direction of degeneration of the relationship. Alcohol provides a quick fix for her bad feelings, which explains, in part, why she turns to it regularly. However, in the long run, drinking alcohol sabotages committed action in the service of her value of intimacy.

In another example, Kim has set up the perfect romantic weekend to celebrate her and Anna's first anniversary. She has planned everything in detail to help get Anna in the mood for romance and sex. Anna considers Kim's preparations a manipulation, however, and feels annoyed and overwhelmed, and she responds by shutting down emotionally and not communicating. Kim, who had great expectations and who has spent much time, money, and energy trying to create a romantic evening, feels extremely disappointed. Thoroughly convinced that Anna has ruined their "special day," Kim walks out angrily and abandons the entire weekend; she looks up a former partner and goes to meet her at a bar, leaving Anna alone on their anniversary.

Kim's case illustrates intolerance for discomfort elicited by rejection. Kim's avoidance strategy is to yield to an impulsive feeling of anger, and then to soothe these negative feelings with the company of other people. Her angry behavior is an effective short-term relief for the negative thoughts and feelings that accompany her perceived rejection, and is validated by social interaction at the bar.

In both the cases just described, short-term reduction of unwanted internal experiences leads to long-term erosion of the vitality of the relationship. The lesson is that avoiding discomfort can lead to more conflict, more distance, or ultimately the end of the relationship.

Avoiding Discomfort Can Lead to Relationship Breakdown

Members of a couple can certainly avoid anxiety, stress, and bad feelings about themselves in the short term, but it may cost them in the long term. In the case of stress and anxiety, for example, using substances can help partners feel more relaxed in the short term; however, substance use can subsequently become habitual and have costs in many valued areas. In addition, even with the relief substances might provide, unwanted internal experiences, such as fear, anxiety, stress, and negative thoughts, aren't likely to go away completely or permanently. In fact, research shows that they actually get worse through such avoidance (Abramowitz, Tolin, & Street, 2001).

It is extremely difficult to get rid of thoughts, fears, memories, and feelings associated with negative psychological events, even for a short time. Hence, people might spend a lot of time and energy trying for the impossible while, in the meantime, their valued life directions may be put on hold, because they believe that getting rid of unpleasant psychological phenomena is a prerequisite for living by their values.

People who have been in an intimate relationship are likely to have significant experience trying to get rid of or solve problems first and *then* proceed in the valued direction. From an ACT perspective, a therapist might ask "How has this worked for you?" The answer in the case of most clients is likely that it has not worked as an overall strategy in the long run. When life in relationships revolves more and more around the reduction of undesired private events and less and less around the pursuit of positive values, then the vitality and the quality of the relationship are diminished. It is worth bearing in mind that when a client voices a wish to get rid of problematic feelings or thoughts, he or she is not simply choosing a conflict-free relationship but expressing a wish for a vital one. The client may say, "I value getting rid of my negative experiences," but the reason, beyond why he or she would want to avoid such bad feelings, is that there is a quality he or she wants in the relationship.

Patterns of Psychological Rigidity in Relationships

In ACT, psychological rigidity is considered the core pathological process. Problematic symptoms and a circumscribed way of living emerge when people habitually engage in particular avoidant behaviors. Robinson, Gould, and Strosahl (2011) have identified fundamental elements of rigidity: living only in the past or future, disconnection with values, being stuck in a self-story, and experiential avoidance. Using a psychotherapy case example, let's look at these four processes in order to understand how these unworkable patterns can become a trap and have devastating consequences for relationships.

Case Study: Ellen

Ellen comes to therapy suffering from her negative thoughts and emotions around excessive spending by her husband, Joe, on items she considers unnecessary. Joe's extravagances have made it difficult to pay the bills. He has promised to control his spending, even working extra hours to pay down their credit-card debt, but Ellen frets that he will not keep his word. She is trapped in ruminating thoughts around themes of his betrayal of her trust, his not caring about her security, and the injustice of her situation. Not only has Ellen's rumination gotten in the way of her acting in a loving manner toward Joe, but she also has trouble concentrating on her work, enjoying herself with friends, and engaging in her own interests. This has led to a depressive state, and she is considering using antidepressants as well as anxiolytics. She has been self-medicating with wine every evening. She has been sleeping badly and neglecting her healthful activities, such as playing tennis and making healthy food.

Following a suggestion by her therapist, Ellen completes a diary of her activities over the course of a week to investigate how she spends her time. The diary shows that she spent three to four hours a day ruminating and just as many hours in behaviors aimed at controlling her anxiety. She spent much time checking Joe's e-mail and credit-card records. She even cut up one of the credit cards that had been sitting in a drawer of his desk. In the evenings, she drank wine to control her anxiety, and this often led to impulsive fighting with Joe.

When asked what she wants to happen in therapy, Ellen answers:

+ "I want Joe to change—to quit his excessive spending."

+ "I want him to show me he loves me."

+ "I want to get back to my life."

Ellen's case provides a typical example of how people can lose track of their valued path—in this case, being a loving, caring partner—and instead actively sabotage an intimate relationship. As Ellen focuses on controlling or eliminating the pain that Joe's spending behavior appears to elicit in her, she starts to lose sight of both her own vital, purposeful life and her valued partnership. She puts her energy into avoidance-based strategies with the intention of controlling her suffering, but in fact, she is clearly increasing her suffering as well as Joe's. In addition, there is a risk that she might continue rigidly in this behavioral pattern until it ultimately contributes to the end of her marriage.

Let's look at the four problematic processes suggested by ACT and see what kind of conceptualization we can make.

Living in the Past or Future

As we mentioned in chapter 4, the vitality of life—specifically, in a relationship—can only be experienced in the "here and now." Suffering in relationships is mainly due to a focus on the past or future. Remember also that pain is inevitable, but suffering is optional. There is just no way to avoid the emotional roller coaster that characterizes a loving relationship; however, long-term suffering endured in the relationship is in fact a mental amplification—created by the sufferer.

Ellen presents her suffering as caused by her partner's past spending and frivolity. Indeed, anyone can understand the pain of a partner's lack of concern about basic household needs. However, initial, understandable pain turns into long-term suffering when people spend more time and energy ruminating about the past or worrying about the future than they spend focused on the present.

Here are some common themes about past grievances.

+ *What if I had been different—would this have happened?*

+ *After all I've done, how could he have done me this injustice?*

+ *I've never been given due credit for my efforts.*

+ *From the very beginning of our relationship, her focus has been on work, not on me.*

People who ruminate over injustices that have been done to them are likely to put themselves through much sadness, anger, and grief. In this way, they experience the present moment through the lens of the past, and it becomes very difficult to contact potentially pleasant experiences available now.

In a similar way, people can be dominated by worry about the future.

+ *After this, I will never trust a lover again.*

+ *People are going to think I am a loser.*

+ *Next time I'll put on a good face and not complain about anything.*

+ *I won't date a lawyer again because they are too consumed with work.*

Worrying about the future elicits anticipatory anxiety or fear.

Here's an example from Ellen's diary showing how her not living in the present moment is sabotaging her relationship.

Today I decided that I really did want to try to get closer to Joe. For once I was not going to complain and bring up how his spending got us in debt, but was going to just stay present. We met at a local restaurant, and things were fine for about five minutes as we looked over the menu. However, when he said he wanted a very expensive item from the menu, that was it! The whole spending issue just came back in a flash. I couldn't control my temper. I called him some name that I really didn't mean and stormed out of the place. Joe never came home that night.

In this example, Ellen and Joe made an attempt to get closer to the intimacy they once had. The context of sitting in a restaurant together offered potential for present-moment intimacy. Joe's menu choice triggered a feeling of insecurity for Ellen. She reacted in a familiarly rigid pattern with a focus on past injustices and her feelings associated with these injustices. The effect of this behavior was a further distancing from intimacy and yet another argument.

Disconnection from Values

With regard to an intimate relationship, values function as a guide or navigation instrument that helps partners stay loving, open, and present regardless of changes in feelings, thoughts, or other content. People who are disconnected from their values may instead follow external rules that substitute for what is personally meaningful. You'll recall from chapter 3 that we called this rule-following behavior "pliance." Here's an example from Ellen's diary that reveals a history of pliance.

> *I grew up in a working-class home with very conservative rules about spending that prioritized necessities. I thought I was liberated from these rules, but after Joe kept buying things that were so expensive and I saw our credit-card debt increasing, I kept thinking that he had violated our sacred trust to take care of each other. I actually spoke to my mother and even my accountant friend about this. They assured me that his behavior was irresponsible. Thinking about these rules helps me feel that I am right and Joe is wrong. But that doesn't help our marriage much.*

Ellen is following socially constructed rules instead of personal values. Although this type of rule-following helps her "feel right" and reduce her discomfort, it leads her away from vitality in her relationship. People who tend to follow rules rather than their own values may be less skilled and flexible in dealing with the complicated problems that can emerge in a long-term, intimate relationship. There are helpful rules and unhelpful rules, but all rules pull people away from the natural contingencies of life. Being on the "right" side of a rule is no substitute for vitality in a relationship. The classic question in ACT is "Is your life going to be about 'being right' or living a vital life?"

Limiting Self-Stories

As we mentioned in chapter 4, who one thinks one is, as well as how one thinks one became who one is, can be either helpful or not helpful in establishing and sustaining an intimate relationship. People write such "stories" about their relationships, too. And, similarly, the stories they write about events in a relationship can be either helpful or harmful for intimacy in that relationship. Remember that there are no literal truths when stories are told, only subjective perspectives. Here are two different ways in which Ellen can tell the story of Joe's spending—one harmful for intimacy, the other helpful for intimacy.

* *Joe really showed me his real self when he spent so much money last year. His complete lack of concern for my security and feelings really taught me that he can't be trusted and that I need to learn not to be so naïve.*

* *Joe has certainly made some bad spending decisions, but I've also bought things that we didn't really need or could have waited to buy. He has spent money on things for the house, such as a new lawnmower and the pretty chandelier for the dining room. He was impulsive, but he was also trying to improve our lives, so I can understand why he wanted these things. I wish he hadn't bought them, but his tendency to be freer with money than I am doesn't need to be a deal-breaker.*

Both of these stories tell of a partner's poor choices. However, they are likely to lead to opposing outcomes.

The first story is likely to sabotage attempts at sustaining intimacy, because its conclusions or rules actually predict future behavior. The message in that story is that Joe's "real self" is someone who is thoughtless and who will continue to be thoughtless. At the same time, Ellen, the creator of the story, predicts that she will behave in a less trusting way. There is identification or fusion with the content of the story: Joe *is* thoughtless and *is* untrustworthy; Ellen *is* naïve. This type of fusion leads to psychological rigidity and is likely to predict future behavior. This is what Robinson and colleagues (2011) refer to as "taking a lower perspective"; that is, Ellen does not see that she is telling a story. Following this perspective is likely to lead her away from intimacy in this relationship—the story's suggestion that Joe is a selfish, thoughtless person to the core doesn't leave much room for the possibility of change for the better. In addition, the suggestion that Ellen needs to change her trusting behavior is not likely to lead to more intimacy.

In the second story, Ellen takes what Robinson et al. (2011) would call "a higher perspective": she sees the story as a story and that it can change. This time, Ellen doesn't identify either herself or Joe with particular character flaws but instead describes a context in which thoughtless behavior was understandable. She is not condoning this behavior, but she understands it in a particular context. This type of story helps her see what needs to change.

When a partner is tied to an identity around a particular self-story, change is very difficult, and conflicts will inevitably arise. The inevitable new behaviors and new situations that arise in a relationship necessitate both partners taking a new perspective on themselves and the relationship. Thus, it is important that partners have a flexible consideration of each other, allowing for the integration of these novel experiences.

Experiential Avoidance

Experiential avoidance, as we have discussed, refers to attempts to control, alter, or escape from distressing private events even to the point where such attempts cause psychological or behavioral harm. An example of experiential avoidance in the context of relationship conflict is impulsive confrontation. Another is withdrawal or noninvolvement in situations that need attention, which might be compounded by a lack of communication or problem-solving skills. Such "stonewalling" is considered a particularly negative behavior, characteristic of couples more likely to separate (Gottman & Silver, 2000).

You might remember that from an ACT perspective, the *form* of a behavior is not as important as its *function*. Essentially any type of behavior may serve to help people avoid their own experiences. Using alcohol or drugs, having sex, sleeping excessively, or withdrawing from valued activities may all fill the function of experiential avoidance—that is, temporary relief from an unpleasant feeling, thought, or memory. In a relationship, people may want to avoid feared situations or challenging or unpleasant interactions. For example, it's common for couples not to talk about areas of disagreement. Here are some additional traps of commonly avoided experiences.

Avoidance of Intimacy

Intimacy is a highly reinforcing or appetitive state for many if not most people. As a result, it is something for which many people yearn. Intimacy is also, ironically, something that many of these same people fear and attempt to avoid, because the highly reinforcing state of intimacy also affords the possibility of the highly punishing experience of rejection, in which one perceives the taking away of his or her sense of belonging and closeness by the other person.

Most people know someone who chooses to live on the safe side, opting to engage in life only when it is comfortable and easy, avoiding experiences that might allow real vitality. Let's consider two examples.

Eve chooses a partner who seems safe and secure rather than a vital partner who might break her heart. She claims that she values intimacy and energetic qualities in relationships, but that she chooses safety instead because the future seems too uncertain, the unknown too disquieting. One of her earliest relationships ended badly and caused her a lot of emotional pain. She remembers that pain and wants to avoid a similar experience.

Charles fears failure so much that he doesn't make any effort to establish an intimate relationship with someone at all. It seems simpler and easier to settle for less than his heartfelt value of intimacy rather than risk diminishment in others' or his own eyes.

Both Eve and Charles are effectively creating a sense of meaninglessness, because though they, in fact, endorse particular values of vital intimacy, they neglect those activities in an attempt to avoid negative experiences.

Pliance

Pliance (introduced in chapter 3) is a kind of rule-governed behavior in which one obeys a rule in order to gain reinforcement from the rule-giver for following the rule. Less technically, pliance could be described as doing things just to please other people. With regard to romantic relationships, choosing a particular partner in order to obtain wider social approval or doing things meant to obtain one's partner's approval are examples of pliance. If the short-term reinforcement of looking good socially or of pleasing one's partner becomes a focus, this is potentially problematic for long-term vitality and psychological health.

Acting to please others, whether one's partner or other important people, may appear to be consistent with long-term valued directions, but functionally it can be very inconsistent with one's values. Pliance is complicated, because people who are in intimate relationships pursue many activities that have some flavor of pliance, and over time they may find that the behavior involved becomes intrinsically reinforcing. For example, coming home in time for dinner might start off as rule-governed, but then it might become intrinsically reinforcing.

If "looking good" and pleasing one's partner is the function of a particular activity, then that activity is technically under the appetitive control of another person's approval. The problem with such a basis of reinforcement is that when no one is around to reinforce that activity, the probably of its occurrence will lessen. For example, you might be less likely to think about your partner or your relationship when your partner is not present. Accordingly, even though your partner loves flowers, you might pass by a florist blindly, not even reflecting that a bouquet would be a nice present. This is an unfortunate feature of pliance that has implications with respect to the establishment of the kinds of lasting patterns of committed action needed for establishing and sustaining vital intimate relationships.

Summary

When people who are in a relationship spend a great deal of time and energy trying to control the uncontrollable, they get stuck in rigid, non-vital patterns, which eventually break down the relationship. In this chapter, we examined a number of different patterns of development of psychological rigidity in relationships. Often prompted by conflict in the relationship, partners can develop unhealthy habitual ways of responding to aversive events.

One way in which psychological inflexibility emerges is when a partner leaves the vitality of the present moment and focuses instead on the past or future. Ruminating about past injustices or worrying about the future is likely to maintain negative feelings and is unhealthy for the relationship.

Disconnecting from personally valued directions for intimate behavior and the relationship and substituting socially constructed rules is another area of possible hazard to vitality. Rigid rule-following, in general, pulls people away from the natural vital contingencies of the present moment and is likely to lead to stagnation.

Another problematic area is getting stuck in limiting and even harmful stories about oneself, one's partner, or both.

Experiential avoidance constitutes a further area of psychological rigidity. This type of behavior is seen in partners who avoid events, situations, and interactions—as well as feelings, physical sensations, memories, or thoughts—that, though potentially unpleasant, need to be approached for the growth of the relationship. Not pursuing intimacy due to a fear of being hurt, as well as doing things to please others (i.e., pliance), reflects experiential avoidance.

Whereas in chapter 5 and the current chapter, we have been examining problematic phenomena, in the next two chapters we consider important health-promoting phenomena in relationships. In the next chapter, we focus on valuing; in chapter 8, we look at self-compassion.

CHAPTER 7

Valuing Intimate Relationships

Introduction

"What do I want in an intimate relationship?" In other words, "What is the function of my relationship for me?" This question is a difficult and complex one, but it is one that people who value intimacy in their relationship need to ask themselves, because the only way to "take the temperature" of an intimate relationship is to know more about its function—what one wants from it; what its meaning or value is. In behavior analysis, RFT, and ACT, understanding and appreciating the function of a behavior is critical with respect to understanding that behavior and predicting its outcome. The function of engaging in an intimate relationship will color (or in RFT terms, transform the stimulus functions of) that whole relationship.

Ideally, the function of an intimate relationship is derived from the fact that a person values the relationship based on his or her experience of the rewards available within it and therefore acts in ways that support, nurture, and develop the relationship so that he or she can continue to enjoy it. However, relationships often have other functions, and these functions may not be conducive to the long-term survival of the relationship or to the psychological health of the people in it.

In this chapter, we consider the theme of valuing in intimate relationships. We consider aspects of valuing in healthy relationships as well as aspects of dysfunctional relationships in which true valuing is absent.

In chapter 4, we presented an ACT definition of values as "freely chosen, verbally constructed consequences of ongoing, dynamic, evolving patterns of activity, which establish predominant reinforcers for that activity that are intrinsic in engagement in the valued behavioral pattern itself" (Wilson & Dufrene, 2009, p. 64).

Let's revisit the concept of valuing, with a particular focus on the valuing of intimate relationships.

Intimate Relationships as Verbally Constructed Consequences

The core of the definition of values is that they are freely chosen verbally constructed consequences of particular types of reinforced activity. People choose particular broadly defined consequences as desirable because those consequences are verbally related to particular types of reinforcement. People's verbal constructions or linguistic descriptions of specific values domains, such as intimacy, are based on their history, as well as on extrapolations from or generalizations about some of the qualities of such experiences. Verbally constructed consequences, such as this, are a core element of what we mean by "values," because they essentially motivate people to act in particular ways (engage in committed action) in order to achieve them.

Intimacy is one such value that many people share. This values domain can be described in terms of sharing one's life experiences with another person. For example, as suggested in chapter 4, if someone is asked to describe what this value involves, he or she might say something like "being able to talk honestly and openly to someone else about my feelings and my experiences." Furthermore, this domain offers several fundamental consequences that are of key importance to human beings—including emotional intimacy, physical closeness, affection, sex, companionship, intellectual stimulation, vitality, meaning, and purpose—and, as such, it is a tremendously important one in terms of psychological sustenance and development.

When people are reminded of a values domain, such as intimacy, they are reminded of the reinforcers available to them in this domain, and they are motivated to engage in activities that keep them oriented toward the domain and toward these reinforcers. This is the RFT concept of motivative augmental control, described in chapter 3 in terms of verbal relational networks that can alter the degree to which previously established consequences function as reinforcers. From an ACT/RFT point of view, the restatement of valued consequences to oneself or others functions as a guide for engaging in certain activities (often neutral or aversive in themselves) that make those reinforcing consequences more likely. The restatement or reminder of values transforms the stimulus functions (in RFT terms) of those activities so that one is more likely to engage in them. With respect to the domain of intimate relationships, there are many such activities that are necessary to the initiation, maintenance, and development of such a relationship.

For example, joining an online dating community and devoting hours of searching and multiple evenings to going on dates with strangers, most of whom you may never see again (and indeed at least some of whom you may hope to never see again!), is not necessarily the most appealing activity, and indeed it might be something that you would in all likelihood avoid if possible. Nevertheless, online dating is an activity in which many millions of people engage, because it offers the possibility of meeting someone with whom they might establish an intimate relationship.

During a relationship, too, potentially difficult emotional issues often come up. For the sake of maintaining and sustaining an honest, healthy intimate relationship, people need to remain open, present, and connected, even during conflicts and other times of stress. Unfortunately, for many people such emotional intimacy can be truly frightening—much more aversive than the typical awkward experiences that might arise in the context of dating, for example—because much more is potentially at stake. Nevertheless, to participate in a truly intimate relationship, it is important that people open up, allowing for feelings of fear and vulnerability.

In these examples, activities that might be neutral and activities that might even be terrifying are described as being needed at times in order to pursue the value of intimacy. People would likely not engage in these activities unless it was necessary to attain the reinforcing consequences (physical closeness, affection, stimulation, vitality, etc.) available within the ambit of this value.

In the following sections, we discuss several key aspects of values in the context of intimate relationships.

Positive Reinforcement in Intimate Relationships

Values are rooted in appetitive stimulation, or positive reinforcement. There are many sources of positive reinforcement in an intimate relationship, as we've stated. Some of these, such as emotional and physical closeness and affection, have their origins very early in life, being typically associated with parental love. Others, such as companionship, intellectual stimulation, and sexual intimacy, gain importance as a child matures and experiences the friendship and love of other people. Sexual intimacy, a particularly powerful source of reinforcement that emerges in adolescence and reaches its fullest expression in early adulthood, is perhaps most centrally associated with the idea and experience of intimate relationships. Ideally, sexual intimacy works closely and harmoniously with physical closeness, affection, and companionship to imbue a relationship with a uniquely powerful dimension of feeling and experience.

In addition to these aspects of relationships, there are the reinforcing qualities of vitality, meaning, and purpose, which derive from the other reinforcers and imbue them with important additional and transformational qualities. Vitality is a primarily emotional experience associated with deliberate engagement in otherwise often neutral or even aversive activities that lead to powerful sources of reinforcement. In an intimate relationship, for instance, you might have feelings of vitality as you deliberately make elaborate and painstaking plans to set up a surprise romantic evening or vacation. Meaning and purpose are related to vitality but are considered to be more abstract verbal concepts associated with working for a greater good (Blackledge & Barnes-Holmes, 2009). In intimate relationships, this greater good might be conceptualized in a number of closely related ways, including a partner's special and unique qualities, as well as the richness of romance and love as a social, human, or possibly even universal phenomenon.

Pursuing Values vs. Pursuing Feelings

As just discussed, vitality is an important dimension of the appetitive quality of reinforcement of values, including intimacy. However, discussion of vitality as an important rein-forcer in this context also brings up a critical issue. We need to make a key distinction and emphasize that vitality, while impor-tant, is a by-product of engaging in committed action in support of one's values. Though vitality or other related positive emo-tional reinforcers are thereby perhaps centrally *theoretically* important to an ACT/RFT understanding of romantic love, people should not mistake them for the value itself and pursue the emotional experience rather than the valued end.

In fact, ACT/RFT would suggest that it is precisely the pursuit of emotions or feelings (e.g., "love") instead of valued ends (e.g., an intimate relationship) that most often causes dis-satisfaction and distress. Furthermore, this is particularly rele-vant in the domain of intimacy, in which emotional experiences play such a central role.

Loving and being loved make people feel good. As discussed, an intimate relationship can be a source of sexual satisfaction and emotional support and can provide a feeling of belonging. These are powerful reinforcers. Indeed, people are inclined to rate the quality of an intimate relationship based on how gener-ally good or happy they feel in that relationship. Furthermore, Western society constantly sends the message that feeling good in all domains of our lives is what we should strive for. For example, the pursuit of happiness (along with life and liberty) is one of the "inalienable rights" mentioned in the US Declaration of Independence (though "happiness" probably meant some-thing different than simply "good feelings" in that context). Conversely, we are taught that feeling bad is something to be avoided and that this is perhaps especially so in relationships, in which neutral or negative feelings are often interpreted as a har-binger of things going wrong.

Given the apparent importance of good and happy feelings, people might infer that achieving such feelings, in fact, constitutes the purpose or intention of being in an intimate relationship. Indeed, given our culture, it is likely that many people do enter into relationships with this attitude, at least implicitly. However, this is a fundamental mistake. Furthermore, it is a mistake that, ironically, results in much less satisfaction and happiness, especially in the medium to long term.

As suggested, feeling good is an important by-product of a psychologically healthy life based on values. However, we disagree with the conventional Western view that pursuit of good feelings or happiness should be seen as a value or end in itself.

Feelings should not be taken as values. Values emerge from relational networks describing particular domains in which long-term sustainable reinforcers are obtainable. People become aware of (i.e., can relationally frame or verbally describe) certain domains as being important to them based on their experience, and when asked about what they value they can name and describe it and can direct their behavior so as to work in congruence with it. In this way, a verbally framed value should act as a lodestone or direction for behavior.

Hence, values should act as a guide or direction in life. Furthermore, feelings of happiness and vitality naturally will arise when people behave in ways that bring them in contact with reinforcers in values domains. However, pursuing feelings as ends in themselves is not something that fits well with this idea of values. This is because, in order to act as a guide, values must be stable. However, feelings are inherently unstable. Emotions, such as feeling good or happy, are a category of behavior referred to as "respondent" or "reflexive." Such behaviors are described as "elicited" as opposed to "emitted" and as relatively involuntary, and they also typically occur relatively quickly and fade away just as quickly. Hence emotions and feelings are involuntary and are relatively ephemeral and fleeting— they come and go. People move between different points in emotional "state space," and they don't have very good control over that movement.

Furthermore, because we humans are verbal creatures, even when we achieve a certain desired emotional state, this state is inherently unstable because, through derived relational responding, we can always imagine the opposite state, or find some reason we might not continue to experience this one. For example, after an intimate moment with your partner, you might think about how happy you are to have him or her—but then begin to think about all the things that might cause your relationship and thus the possibility of this happiness to end, which might change your emotional state.

As we have explained, there is no doubt that feelings are a core part of an intimate relationship. Living in accordance with values results in feelings of vitality. For example, engaging in activities meant to maintain a strong, well-founded relationship will tend to be characterized by good feelings (e.g., vitality, love, and happiness). But an intimate relationship, even a healthy one, can of course also be a source of aversive emotional experiences. Expectations are not always met, feelings are constantly changing, and rejection in some form may be a daily occurrence. Hence, sometimes people will feel happy in their relationship and deeply committed to their partner; sometimes they won't feel quite as strongly; and, at other times, they may feel very sad or angry. Also, in relationships, just as in any other context, people don't always have control over exactly when they have one type of feeling versus another.

Hence, we would suggest that, when it comes to the choice of consistent, overarching values or directions in life, the pursuit of particular types of feelings as ends in themselves does not make sense and will ultimately result in frustration, confusion, and psychological problems. This is true for intimacy as well as other domains. Indeed, it may even be more so in this domain, because feeling and emotion play such a large part in it, and, of course, it is not just the feelings of one person that are involved but those of two.

In summary, achieving particular types of feelings, whether good or otherwise, should not be seen as the value underlying or reason for having a relationship. Instead, the value is best described as the intimate relationship itself; powerful reinforcers that sustain commitment to this value include affection and physical and intellectual stimulation. By behaving in ways that sustain and nurture their relationship, people who value intimacy and are in an intimate relationship are living in accordance with their value and helping sustain that value for the long term.

Historical Evidence Concerning Feelings-Based Intimacy

Thus far, we have argued that if the unstable and ephemeral experience of "feeling good" is people's main intention in a relationship, then that relationship is likely to lose vitality and degenerate over time. Now, let's look at some historical evidence concerning pursuit of feelings as opposed to values.

Coontz (2005) asserts that throughout most of human history, marriage, partnership, and family have been based on values rather than mediated by feelings such as personal happiness or love. The idea of basing marriage on personal feelings arose as recently as the 1850s, and Coontz shows how this very idea led to the downfall of marriage as an institution. She argues that no sooner had the idea of love-based marriage begun than people began demanding the right to divorce once they felt as though they were no longer in love. Between 1870 and 1890, divorces in the Western world increased by 70 percent. This is an example of moving from values-based intimacy (i.e., engaging in behaviors because they coincide with a valued direction) to feelings-based intimacy (i.e., engaging in behaviors based on experiences of love as an emotion). Public criticism of "love-based" marriages documented in the late 1800s and early 1900s was rooted in the concern that basing society's most important intimate relationship on the notion of the achievement of perpetual happiness for those involved was a recipe for disaster. As we have discussed, feelings do change; and it could be argued that, in accordance with the warning from those supporting the more traditional, values-based conception of marriage, the switch to personal feelings as the arbiter of the quality of a marriage probably did contribute to the downfall of marriage as an institution.

Coontz points out that in many countries, such as Sweden, marriage has lost many of its former functions (e.g., social and legal functions), and as a result, other options, such as single-parent families and cohabitation, have become more common than traditional, marriage-based families. Of course, the fact that traditional marriage has changed in its societal form, role, or importance in particular societies and Western society more generally is not news, is not necessarily a bad thing, and indeed may even be argued to be a good thing, to the extent that it has allowed greater choice for a greater variety of people. The key point here is that Coontz's historical perspective sheds some light on how a change in function from a basis in values to a basis in feelings can affect people's behavior. More specifically, it suggests that seeking feelings-based fulfillment can dissolve relationships relatively readily. And to the extent that such relationships might otherwise have survived and become sources of true, values-based contentment, seeking feelings-based fulfillment can lead to an increase in suffering. We are not suggesting, however, that historically all marriages based on social standing or family arrangements were devoid of suffering; nor are we advocating such arrangements as superior to the current Western custom of personal choice when it comes to intimate relationships.

For most people, wanting to be happy or to pursue happiness is ingrained. "Happiness" feels good and, at least in North America, tends to be high on lists of what people value (Diener, 2000; Myers, 2000). However, there is emerging empirical evidence to suggest that the pursuit and experience of happiness might sometimes lead to negative outcomes. In one study, Schooler, Ariely, and Loewenstein (2003) found that participants instructed to make themselves as happy as possible while listening to music reported feeling less happy compared to no-instruction controls. Mauss, Tamir, Anderson, and Savino (2011) report two studies of more direct relevance to the issue of valuing happiness and good feelings more generally. In a correlational study, they found that valuing happiness correlated negatively with well-being and positively with mental health difficulties, including depression. In an experimental study, they found that participants induced to value happiness (by reading a newspaper article that suggested the advantages of feeling happy) felt worse than a control group, according to both implicit and explicit assessments of their emotional state, after watching a "happy" film clip, apparently because they felt disappointed that they had not managed to feel happier while watching it.

These studies provide empirical evidence that the pursuit of "feeling good" as a value is problematic. Recent work reported by Mauss et al. (2012) is of particular relevance to the valuing of good feelings in the context of relationships. In a correlational study, these authors found that the more people valued happiness, the higher their daily reported levels of loneliness (as recorded in an experimental diary). In an experimental study, the same authors showed that inducing people to value happiness led to higher levels of loneliness and social disconnect (based on self-report as well as levels of progesterone) and lower levels of well-being.

Hence, people who value happiness may experience decreased social connection and ultimately loneliness, which, in turn, is one of the most robustly *negative* predictors of happiness and well-being (J. T. Cacioppo, Hughes, Waite, Hawkley, & Thisted, 2006; Steverink & Lindenberg, 2006). On the other hand, there is research to suggest that people who define happiness less in terms of positive feelings (e.g., those with Asian cultural backgrounds, as discussed in Uchida, Norasakkunkit, & Kitayama, 2004) show weaker or even reversed effects of valuing happiness on loneliness.

One possible conclusion is that when people place high value on personal outcomes, whether it be having high self-esteem, being right, being successful, or being happy, they might be more concerned with themselves and less concerned with others, which leads to increased feelings of loneliness. Wanting to be happy may have opposite effects than "being happy," and often leads to negative social outcomes. In other words, desiring to be happy is very different behavior than actually acting in a "happy" manner, and has different consequences.

The evidence above can be supplemented by a more basic or generalized ACT/RFT perspective on why seeking happiness might lead to more negative emotion. Our earlier discussion of the nature of values has already hinted at possible processes from this point of view. Basically, if experiencing and sustaining a particular feeling is person's criterion for success, then he or she will likely never achieve that success. We can think of this as an example of rule-following in which the rule is "I must feel happy." In order to follow this rule, people must check every so often to see that they are indeed feeling happy. However, feelings are ephemeral and subject to change, and so people may well be feeling some emotion other than happiness at the time they do their emotional check. In addition, even if they do happen to be feeling relatively happy when they check their emotional state, language allows people to make comparisons between that state and other possible states (e.g., past states, imagined future states, and imagined states of others), and those comparisons can then transform the stimulus functions of the present and change their emotional state. For example, people might derive "Yes, I'm relatively happy, but I was happier in the past," or "Yes, I'm happy now, but when I get X, I'll be so much happier." This applies to intimate relationships just as it does other contexts. For example, in the midst of physical or emotional intimacy with your partner, you might derive the relation "My partner might leave me." This would temporarily transform the stimulus functions of your partner ("someone who can cause me pain") and of the situation ("one that is temporary and might be followed by aversive feelings at some point in the future"). This RFT analysis constitutes a relatively broad explanation for why the pursuit of happy feelings is not conducive to long-term satisfaction and why this is true in intimate relationships as in other contexts.

Choosing Intimacy as a Value

The first phrase in Wilson and DuFrene's (2009) definition of valuing is "freely chosen." As discussed in chapter 4, what this phrase means is that people's choice of values should be free from aversive control. Essentially, people feel freer when acting to produce positive consequences than when trying to avoid or escape aversive ones. An intimate relationship that enriches may feel more freely chosen than one that functions as a relief from loneliness, for example. It may seem as if this does not go beyond the previous feature of values being appetitive. However, there are degrees of appetitive versus aversive control. There can be relatively appetitive activities that are nonetheless rooted in choices made by someone else (e.g., engaging in a rewarding career that was originally chosen based on parental advice or societal influence) or appetitive sources of control that start as powerfully appetitive but result in increasing levels of aversive control (e.g., psychoactive drugs). In this way, there can be a mixture of appetitive and aversive control. Thus, there can be both positively and negatively reinforcing aspects of intimate relationships.

For example, in the last chapter we discussed how language can create a narrative of self-deficiency that remains fairly consistent from an early age. This story of deficiency or of "being less" is something that people often go to great lengths to avoid, and one key domain that offers the possibility of engaging in such avoidance is intimacy.

Here are some typical examples of what people say when asked why they are seeking an intimate relationship:

+ "I feel lonely without someone in my life."

+ "I am looking for security."

+ "I am looking for my other half."

+ "I want to be with someone I can trust."

+ "I want to feel happy."

It could be argued that in all of these examples, avoidance is, for the speaker, a core function of an intimate relationship. All of these statements suggest that the speaker lacks something, something that he or she hopes that some other person will be able to supply. The idea is that once the speaker has met this other person, the speaker will no longer have to cope with his or her deficiency as manifested in feelings of loneliness, sadness, or insecurity. However, this view of intimate relationships is fundamentally problematic, and a relationship founded on avoidance in this way will ironically be very likely to lead to even more severe problems of the kind that it was used initially to avoid.

In contrast with the above, consider the following examples:

+ "I enjoy sharing my time with another person."

+ "I find negotiating the joys and difficulties of a close relationship to be stimulating."

+ "I like the give-and-take of emotional and physical intimacy."

+ "I enjoy routines and familiarity."

In these examples, the function of establishing intimacy is very different from avoidance of deficiency: in each case, the speaker is expressing the pursuit of something that will add to his or her life in a positive or reinforcing way. For a relationship to be healthy, its core function should be the pursuit of rein-forcement, as opposed to the avoidance of punishment. To reit-erate: ideally, people's choice of values should be as free of aversive control as possible.

A relationship's freedom from aversive control is probably best indicated by the presence of the vitality, meaning, and purpose we discussed a bit earlier. For example, consider the following statements:

+ "I tried every shop in the city to find that gift; I just wanted to see the joy on her face."

+ "Those intimate conversations about everything and nothing are one of my deepest joys."

+ "My relationship with him has truly inspired me and enriched my life."

When people describe their relationship in terms of strong positive emotions derived from engaging in otherwise aversive or taxing activities meant to support their relationship (i.e., vitality), or in terms of the meaning and purpose that it gives them in life, this indicates a strong and healthy relationship that is almost the opposite of one involving strong aversive qualities.

Intimacy: Intrinsic and Long-Term Sustainable Reinforcement

Reinforcers that are contacted through committed action are typically both intrinsic and long-term sustainable (sustainable over the long term). These qualities are the key to why such reinforcers can support valuing over the course of a lifetime. The previously discussed reinforcers in the domain of intimacy—emotional intimacy, physical closeness, affection, sex, companionship, intellectual stimulation, vitality, meaning, and purpose—include several sources of reinforcement that might be classified in this way.

The term "intrinsic" was explicitly mentioned in the definition of valuing used earlier (from Wilson & Dufrene, 2009) in reference to the reinforcing qualities of particular activities. It highlights the fact that the reinforcement comes from the activity itself rather than from some outside ("extrinsic") source. In general, the greater the extent to which people pursue and contact intrinsic reinforcement, the more likely that they are living a life consistent with their values.

What intimate behaviors are considered intrinsically reinforcing? Activities yielding primary reinforcement, such as sexual arousal and physical touch, might classically be categorized as intrinsically reinforcing, because people are biologically primed to derive reinforcement from them. Because we are a verbal species, however, we find many activities related (sometimes directly and sometimes less so) to these sources of primary reinforcement to be intrinsically reinforcing also. In fact, due to language, much of what we find intrinsically reinforcing is quite arbitrary, far from based on immediate biological processes. In the context of romance, for example, giving or receiving love poetry, marriage vows, and daily verbal expressions of love are activities that could be considered intrinsically reinforcing, but their psychological effect is not based on simple biology. Instead, their capacity for intrinsic reinforcement has its basis in people's verbal history and involves reinforcement through transformation of stimulus functions which, in turn, is ultimately rooted in more basic biological processes. As a result of the verbal connection, people are likely to describe such reinforcers as pleasurable and meaningful.

Activities that are intrinsically reinforcing will likely be sustainable over the long term. While the reinforcers found in the domain of intimacy may differ to some degree in this respect (for example, sexual intimacy loses its potency over time), all of them are at least potentially long-term sustainable to some degree. Long-term sustainability of valued activities is particularly important, because values are long-term life directions. In general, the types of reinforcement to be found through pursuit of values should amount to more than thrills. For example, the emotional highs associated with the early stages of a relationship can seem all-consuming, especially to someone with little or no experience of relationships. However, these highs almost invariably do not last; once they start to fade, one or both partners may become bored and want to move on, which, at a minimum, is unsatisfying for both people, and could be quite painful for a partner who had been prepared to commit more fully. Healthy relationships should provide and come to be associated with long-term sustainable sources of reinforcement for both partners, ideally including all of those sources described previously—not just emotional and physical intimacy, but also affection, companionship, intellectual stimulation, vitality, meaning, and purpose. Of course, the degree to which people can pursue and remain in contact with these reinforcers over time will vary.

The Values Hierarchy: Healthy and Unhealthy Valuing Behavior

RFT allows us to conceptualize a values domain in terms of a hierarchical relational network, at the top of which is the value itself. Next are those long-term, sustainable, intrinsically reinforcing phenomena, such as those named in the preceding paragraph, that contribute directly to that value. Lower nodes in the network include supporting (extrinsic) activities that offer access to those core reinforcers. For instance, in the domain of intimacy, lower nodes might include having a job and making money to support oneself and one's partner.

Visualizing values in this way (i.e., in terms of hierarchies), it is possible to conceptualize both healthy and maladaptive behavior with respect to valued activity. Clearly, engagement in long-term sustainable valued activity, such as seen at the pinnacle of the hierarchy, is psychologically healthy from our perspective, and the more time one spends in such activity across a number of values domains, the better. With respect to intimacy, this means that physical closeness—including sexual activity and sharing experiences, for example—is obviously tremendously psychologically valuable. At the same time, investing in activities lower on the hierarchy is also important because it allows access to the activities at the top of the hierarchy. Investing in activities deliberately to support core values, such as relationships, is healthy and can be categorized as valuing. For example, working at your job to make money for your partner and yourself would be seen as valuing your relationship;

indeed, as we described earlier, it might be vitalizing, particularly if working at your job might otherwise be aversive but you are doing it in conscious support of your value.

Patterns of behaviors that are healthy for a relationship entail this pinnacle of intrinsically reinforcing valued behavior, with more extrinsically reinforcing activities farther down. However, if an imbalance arises in the hierarchy such that more extrinsically reinforced activities, such as gaining money or status or working to please a partner, come to gain control over behavior, there may be problems. This may occur in the context of fusion with rules about the importance of money and other socially conventional reinforcement; people may come to invest time and energy in activities that produce such reinforcement—originally intended as means to ends—at the expense of long-term sustainable intrinsically reinforcing activities. Such people might speak about marriage status or economic security as values. This is referred to as *fusion with outcome*. Such fusion can obviously undermine a relationship, causing it to lose vitality, because there is simply less time for the valued intimate behaviors that make a relationship worthwhile.

The same activity might be functionally very different, depending on the intention and context. Take making money or getting married, for example. On the one hand, making money or getting married can be functionally healthy and vital to the relationship if it supports the core valued activity of caring for oneself and one's partner. On the other hand, making money or getting married can be functionally problematic if it is seen as an end in itself, and the time and effort invested in activities that allow for making money or planning a wedding have no valued end in sight and take precedence over potentially vitalizing valued activity.

There is also the possibility of people making money or getting married because of social expectations or because their parents or friends have specifically pressured them to do so. This influence may be the basis of a more fundamental problem than that in the preceding example, and thus there may perhaps be a more urgent need to address it, for the sake of the relationship and the psychological health of both partners.

Unhealthy Influences on Valuing in Relationships

One reason people might prize socially constructed reinforcement over intrinsic reinforcement is sociocultural programming.

As discussed in chapter 4, values develop within a socioverbal context. The verbal community shapes people's statements about what is "good" or "bad," what is important, and what is desirable, including with respect to relationships. For example, parents or caregivers introduce their children to others who might be appropriate playmates or friends; media and the commercial world present romantic stories and images of celebrities that influence concepts of desirability. Over time people develop ideas about what they want, their purpose, and a direction for their lives, including images and statements about the perfect partner.

One thing that people may come to prize based on such social influence is physical attractiveness in a partner. Although the reinforcing power of physical attractiveness is no doubt based in human biology, and attractiveness is legitimately important and valued, it is important that young people also learn and come to appreciate the importance of other qualities in potential partners. In particular, many of the long-term sustainable sources of reinforcement in a relationship do not depend on physical attractiveness. Too much emphasis on attractiveness might overshadow or obscure the importance of other qualities available in a partner.

People are taught to prize other potential distractors as well. Our society prizes such secondary reinforcers in relationships as engagement rings, wedding ceremonies, money, and status. Here, again, the function is of primary importance. A diamond ring, a wedding, money, and status might be seen as means to a higher end, but people who are fused with rules concerning the importance of social affirmation may come to see these arbitrary markers as ends in themselves.

Downplaying Relationship Values

The effect of sociocultural influences in emphasizing extrinsic reinforcement and downplaying the value of intrinsically reinforcing activities in relationships may be compounded by the effects of particular familial environments in which expression of interest in intrinsically reinforcing activities is suppressed. Children expressing wants or needs might, under certain circumstances, be met with punishing reactions (e.g., ignoring, ridiculing, or aggression) from parents, siblings, or significant others.

For example, a young girl in a conservative household who expresses interest in a traditionally masculine activity might be ignored or even ridiculed and might henceforward be less likely to express this potential value. In this way, intrinsically reinforcing activity and, ultimately, "valuing" might be diminished to some degree by the social context. As another example, consider a young boy who finds himself attracted to members of his own gender. As a result of social contingencies, including the provision of approval for heterosexual behavior and the provision of disapproval—including, perhaps, aversive emotional and physical consequences—for homosexual behavior, he might deliberately repress these feelings, which would otherwise constitute the basis of a core dimension of the value of intimate relationship for him.

As young children, we all learn behavior to please others (i.e., pliance). In some cases, however, particularly in environments in which expressions of their own wants and needs are consistently punished, children never really learn to move past the stage of doing what others tell them to do or acting in line with what others expect of them. If, as in the above examples, children's expressions of their wants and needs are consistently met with punishing reactions, then they simply learn to suppress those wants and needs in order to avoid punishment. Children who are neglected are especially likely to express diminished values, having come to associate potential valued directions with pain, punishment, abandonment, and disappointment. Children whose caregivers are frequently intoxicated with alcohol or drugs, for example, may have their needs and wants ignored and as a consequence may not learn to express what is important to them. Children who are abused are likely to have significant aversive conditioning associated with valued intimate behavior: those who are physically abused are likely to associate parents, adults, and caretakers with violence and the threat of violence, while those who are sexually abused may associate physical closeness and words of love with force and violence.

For clients in therapy who have this type of abusive learning history, identifying highly valued behaviors and developing intimacy may take some time. The value or example of wanting to establish a warm, loving relationship may be present, but there may also be a long history of painful experiences associated with relationships. Asking the client to connect to deeply held values in love relationships may well elicit memories of these painful experiences. In fact, due to aversive conditioning, some people may try to avoid or sabotage relationships they actually value. If "valuing" is associated with punishment, this may in part explain why values are diminished and thus effectively avoided.

Intimacy and Variety in Values Domains

Intimacy is just one of a number of values domains, of course, and in general the more values domains in which people engage, the better it is for their psychological health and for their pursuit of values in any particular domain. Therefore, having a variety of values outside of one's romantic relationship is very likely to support and sustain the relationship, too.

The more sources of long-term positive reinforcement that are available to people, the less likely they are to become overly dependent on any one source. In other words, it is important that intimacy not be their only value. Ideally, people should establish and maintain a balance between different natural reinforcers in a variety of life dimensions. Pursuing intimacy or any other single source of reinforcement exclusively will pull people away from all the other valued directions that they may follow in the present moment. Valuing only intimacy, and especially valuing their current relationship as the only possible one, will considerably narrow people's behavioral repertoire and make them dependent on the relationship, such that they are at risk of trauma if anything threatens it. Furthermore, such narrowed valuing will likely negatively affect the quality of the relationship (perhaps by prompting "needy" behavior), thus itself threatening the relationship.

In addition, valuing intimacy can be supported by the activities involved in valuing other domains. There can, of course, be potential overlap in terms of different values domains and valued activities. In the case of intimacy, there are potentially important contributions from other domains, such as health and socializing. Activities that pertain to these domains, such as exercising, eating, sleeping, and maintaining friendships and engagement in social groups, are psychologically important in themselves as well as supportive of the domain of intimacy, because they support one's attractiveness as a potential or continued partner.

Furthermore, the importance of variety pertains not just across values dimensions but also within them. Early in a relationship, people sometimes pursue a narrow range of reinforcement based on intimacy (e.g., primarily sexual activities), which can lead to satiation and disappointment; it is important that other aspects of the relationship (e.g., companionship, affection, and intellectual stimulation) be cultivated also. This point has been made before in other ways (such as in the previous section), but it is important to remember it.

Intimacy as a Value: Some Additional Points

Before we conclude this chapter on valuing intimacy, we refer to some potentially important additional points about values, and discuss how these points are relevant specifically in relation to intimate relationships.

Values Can Never Be Attained

Values are described in ACT/RFT as chosen, verbally constructed consequences. As discussed in chapter 4, values can never be fulfilled but instead function as motivation for certain behavioral directions. In chapter 4 we illustrated this using the example of caring within an intimate relationship. As indicated, in this context, the value of caring is shown by such behaviors as sharing personal information or asking about the other person's day, which aren't about fulfilling concrete goals but instead are behaviors in the direction of the value.

Despite this, outcomes, achievements, status, physical beauty, an engagement ring, and a marriage certificate (i.e., goals) are, in fact, marketed as values in love relationships. In order to shape and maintain consumer behavior, advertisers deliberately make goals look like values. Wedding planners, jewelry stores, and flower shops all advertise consumption of their products as an act of love, in the same way that the marketing efforts of cosmetics companies imply to women that use of their products equates to valuing themselves.

One way to illustrate the distinction between values and goals is to use the metaphor of the compass (see, e.g., Hayes et al., 1999; Dahl, Plumb, Stewart, & Lundgren, 2009). Taking a valued direction is like navigating by compass. Once we decide on our direction, we can immediately step into our full course with just the slightest movement and we are right on target. Important for people who are goal-oriented to understand is that one never actually *gets to* one's direction. One never arrives. For example, you can go east or west your whole life and never arrive at an end point. Values, unlike goals, can never be fully achieved.

Goals in relationships (as in other values-relevant domains) are different from valued directions. Goals are waypoints on the set course, such as establishing exclusivity, getting engaged, moving in together, and getting married. They are practical, are quantifiable, and have clear beginning and end points. These waypoints can help people orient themselves along the course that they have set. Once a goal has been reached, however, it loses its value as a waypoint and a new goal must be set. Once a couple have gone through a marriage ceremony, for example, then new waypoints must be added in order to maintain the valued direction of the relationship. For example, a new goal might be creating a routine that carves out time on a daily basis for reconnecting with each other. The purpose of creating such goals is to keep couples on track in the course of the valued intimate behavior but not replace the valued direction.

Values Are Rules—but Following Them Is Broadly Defined

Values, if taken literally, can be viewed as statements of truth or rules to which we must adhere. However, while technically they are rules, these rules are freely chosen and do not prescribe any particular behaviors. In chapter 4 we gave an example of someone being nurturing in relationships and said that even though someone might have this value of being nurturing, this alone would not indicate precisely how he or she should engage in nurturing behaviors (e.g., how frequently or with whom). We suggested that values as rules simply orient people to general patterns of purposeful behavior that should ideally be meaningful and reinforcing, but that people must learn how to choose behaviors that accord with those values based on their own experience. This indicates, in addition, that flexibility is important for living in accordance with one's values. For example, while one's values might stay the same, the kinds of behaviors that embody those values might change in form over the years in response to different life circumstances.

Summary

In this chapter, we discussed important aspects of intimacy as a value. We started with a reminder of the definition of valuing and then explored key aspects of that definition with regard to intimacy as a value, including (1) relationships as verbally constructed consequences, focusing on the RFT concept of valuing as augmental control and how this idea pertains to intimacy; (2) sources of positive reinforcement within relationships, including an in-depth consideration of the contrast between the pursuit of values as constructed consequences linked to long-term sustainable reinforcers and the pursuit of particular types of feelings (short-term reinforcers); (3) the choice of intimacy as a value, and what it means to choose "freely"; (4) the concept of intrinsic and long-term sustainable reinforcement as it pertains to valuing within relationships, including consideration of the values hierarchy; and (5) some additional points concerning the nature of valuing, including the fact that values can never be attained and the categorization of values as rules.

In the next chapter, we examine how compassion for oneself is an important component of authentic compassion toward others, particularly one's partner, and thus how self-compassion serves as a basis for relationships.

CHAPTER 8

Self-Compassion

+ Introduction

+ Definition of Self-Compassion

+ ACT Processes Supporting Self-Compassion

+ Summary

Introduction

We might describe a healthy intimate relationship as two people relating to each other in a way that enriches, vitalizes, and provides meaning to them both as individuals and as a couple. A key aspect of such a relationship is compassion for the other person. However, from an ACT/RFT perspective, compassion toward other people might be expected to correlate with and be supported by compassion toward oneself. As such, an important foundation of compassion for one's partner would be self-compassion as we assume in this chapter. Here, we aim to describe the foundations of a healthy relationship from an ACT/RFT perspective. We suggest that there are two prerequisites for a healthy relationship: (1) acting in the valued direction of self-compassion and (2) acting in the valued directions of love and compassion toward one's partner.

Definition of Self-Compassion

Self-compassion involves the extension of kindness, love, and understanding to one's own pain and suffering. It allows one to respond appropriately to his or her own distress with warmth and caring, instead of self-criticism or self-pity. Neff (2003) has suggested that self-compassion involves self-kindness, mindfulness, and recognition that suffering is part of the human condition.

RFT provides a basic conceptualization of compassion at the level of psychological process. In chapter 3, we discussed a number of phenomena relevant to compassion. These included (1) empathy and (2) the verbal other.

Processes Involved in Compassion

The RFT conception of empathy involves the transformation of emotional functions via deictic relations. People "feel for" another person when, through deictic framing, they experience psychological functions of the other's situation. Thus, as children become increasingly capable of deictic relational framing—in particular, transformation of emotional functions through deictic frames—they become increasingly capable of engaging in empathic responding with respect to others.

Thus, in developmental terms, at least, feeling for oneself precedes feeling for other people. This is a key foundation of empathy. People need to be able to feel certain emotions (e.g., fear or sadness) in order to empathize with someone else who might be feeling those emotions. If people can't feel those emotions, then they won't feel empathy. However, if people can feel emotions, they can use I-YOU perspective-taking—framing in which they "put themselves in another's situation"—combined with transformation of emotional functions, to feel the emotions that others are feeling, too.

The verbal other is also relevant. As discussed in chapter 3, RFT proposes three types of verbal other: other-as-content, other-as-process, and other-as-context. Other-as-content refers to framing the kind of person the other is; other-as-process refers to framing the ongoing experience of the other; and other-as-context refers to framing the other as pure perspective. Other-as-process seems immediately relevant to empathy, because empathy is about sharing the experience of another person, and contact with the experience of another is typically based on a construction of that experience, which is other-as-process. Contacting the pain and suffering of another through the present-focused other-as-process allows feelings of compassion and sympathy to arise as a natural contingency. In addition, other-as-context is relevant—maybe particularly so—in facilitating compassion.

Variables Affecting Compassion

Once children become capable of empathy based on transformation of emotional functions via deictic relations, they might in addition learn to act to alleviate others' distress. People experiencing empathy may act to alleviate another person's distress for a variety of reasons—for example, to alleviate their own distress; because of social rules about what to do when other people are in distress; to act in accordance with their values (e.g., if they value helping other people or society more generally); or some combination of these.

It seems likely that a particularly important variable affecting whether an empathic feeling will lead people to try to alleviate another's distress is mindfulness. Mindfulness is based on the concepts of self-as-context and other-as-context, which were defined in chapter 3 in terms of perspective alone (as simply particular points of view). In other words, mindfulness involves stripping away any idiosyncrasies that might make people different from each other, and thus it offers maximum opportunity for seeing others as the same as oneself; hence, if people are motivated to help themselves, then they will also be motivated to help others, because the two are the same in this context. Contacting the self as a point of pure perspective in the absence of the influence of rules may also make people more motivated to work to alleviate their own distress, because being stripped of content means losing transformations of negative functions in regard to oneself that might otherwise make one less likely to act. The combination of these elements makes it more likely that one would help another person also.

Thus we might say that there are two important ways in which compassion for others is supported by feeling compassion for oneself. First, in order to feel what another feels as a result of transformation of functions through deictic relations, one needs to have experienced a similar situation. Second, in order to act compassionately toward another based on feeling the same, and thus becoming motivated to help, one needs to feel motivated to help oneself. In addition, however, ACT/RFT would suggest that an important aspect of becoming motivated to help both oneself and others is experience of self-as-context.

Failure of Compassion

Just as this analysis suggests how mindfulness/self-as-context can support the link between feeling for oneself and feeling for another, it indicates that this link can be broken, especially in a context of fusion or lack of mindfulness. For example, there are obviously times when people feeling another's pain through deictic framing might act simply to alleviate their own distress as opposed to the other person's. They might do so by attempting to avoid the distress in some way other than by actually helping the person (e.g., through distortion, distraction, or suppression of the experience, or by avoiding similar situations thereafter). They might be more likely to do this if the distress seems especially pronounced, perhaps as a result of fusion with rules suggesting that they are unable to cope with the experience.

There is also the possibility for people to be overly concerned with other people's welfare while disregarding their own. This is likely also caused by fusion with unhelpful rules, such as "I am unworthy" or "I am not good enough." Alternatively, such people might be acting in accordance with a religious rule, such as "If I help other people first before myself, then ultimately that will help me get into heaven." It could also be that helping others is negatively reinforced by avoidance of guilt: for example, in accordance with the rule "If I don't help others before myself, then I am a bad person."

In both of these cases, there appears to be a breakdown in the system whereby someone who is in need (either one person or the other) is being neglected. ACT/RFT would suggest the importance of mindfulness/self-as-context here. From the perspective of mindfulness/self-as-context, compassion for oneself and compassion for others are naturally linked and support each other, but this link is moderated by the level of mindfulness. If one is behaving mindfully, then the transformation of functions between I and YOU happens readily (assuming other appropriate contextual control that allows discrimination between the two states [I and YOU] and thus allows acting appropriately based on who, according to the evidence, is actually in need). On the other hand, if one is fused with unhelpful rules, as in the preceding paragraphs, compassion and self-compassion may be artificially divorced.

Hence, appropriate action in accordance with feelings works best in a context of mindfulness. From an ACT/RFT point of view, mindfulness is a product of self-as-context or self-awareness. One key way in which people can become self-aware is through deliberate exercises in self-compassion. By practicing self-compassion, people can gain insight into themselves and improve their psychological health while making it more likely that they will develop genuine and sustainable empathy for others, including their partner in an intimate relationship.

Empirical Support for the Importance of Self-Compassion

ACT research (e.g., Hayes, et al. 2004; Lillis et al., 2010; Luoma, O'Hair, Kohlenberg, Hayes, & Fletcher, 2010; Luoma et al., 2007; Masuda et al., 2007; Masuda et al., 2009; Yadavaia & Hayes, 2012) shows that when therapists are trained to express self-compassion, both they and their clients do much better. These studies show that non-self-compassionate behavior is correlated with non-compassionate behavior toward others. It also has been demonstrated that self-compassionate behavior is correlated with compassion toward others. Indeed, Neff and Beretvas (2012) demonstrated that people who rated high in self-compassion exhibited more positive behaviors in their relationships. Further, Yarnell and Neff (2013) found that self-compassion was associated with a greater likelihood of compromise during conflicts and also promoted feelings of authenticity, resulting in less emotional turmoil and higher levels of emotional well-being.

This research on self-compassion also suggests that members of a couple who do not act with self-compassion toward themselves are not likely to act in a loving, kind manner toward their partner. Consequently, those who learn self-compassion skills are more likely to be effective in showing compassion for their partner. It follows that self-compassion might be a very important ingredient of healthy relationships, one that helps partners establish and maintain vital intimacy.

ACT Processes Supporting Self-Compassion

Hayes (2008) presents the ACT perspective on self-compassion, positing a number of key ACT processes that support compassion and self-compassion:

+ Embracing difficult feelings

+ Observing difficult and judgmental thoughts without entanglement

+ Connecting with a spiritual sense of self that transcends this programming

+ Carrying one's history forward into a life of compassionate engagement in self-validation

Self-compassion is not a *feeling*, as we can see by the above definition; rather, it consists of patterns of behaviors. Self-compassion could also be described as accepting or loving oneself—not in an egotistical kind of way, but in a way that is reflective of caring for everyone, universally. We are considering the patterns or processes involved in self-compassion listed above as occurring in a sequence, and hence in the following examination of them we refer to them as "steps." Of course, in reality the processes will overlap in time, and there will also be "back and forth" between them. Nevertheless, in a relatively approximate or loose way, they can be thought of as steps in a sequence.

Embracing Difficult Feelings

In chapter 3, we discussed the tendency to want to avoid negative feelings and thoughts, known as experiential avoidance. Self-compassion entails an active, loving, patient embracing of difficult feelings. This process of responding kindly to pain involves several behaviors.

People often become aware of their difficult feelings through physical sensations of the "fight, flight, or freeze" response: that activation of the sympathetic nervous system (for most people, a characteristic chain of events that starts with an increase in breathing, followed by increased heart rate, muscle tension, and so on) that means that the body is reacting to a perceived threat (an aversive stimulus or unpleasant event) and is readying itself to either resist and defend against or avoid it. The first act of self-compassion in these circumstances is just to notice that the body is reacting to some private event (i.e., thought or emotion) in a non-accepting or avoiding manner. Embracing these reactions might mean simply breathing normally and making room for any sensations, feelings, or thoughts that are present without further reaction to them. In other words, one allows for whatever is happening internally, without feeding or reinforcing those reactions with further mental amplification or physical resistance. This involves opening up and approaching conditioned reactions rather than avoiding them. Steps in self-compassionate behavior can include becoming aware of bodily chain reactions and being moved by one's own suffering.

Below, we introduce Lisa, who is having difficulty establishing intimate relationships, and show how ACT might help her develop self-compassionate behavior as a prerequisite to developing intimate behavior with others. We use the example of Lisa for the remainder of this chapter to illustrate the concepts we discuss.

> Lisa, age thirty-one, identifies as bisexual. She has actively dated (mostly men), but she has never managed to sustain a long-term relationship. She wants to have children but is beginning to doubt that this will ever happen, because none of her relationships has lasted more than a few months, and she doesn't want to raise a child on her own. Lisa has noticed that as soon as she starts to feel insecure or uncertain in a new relationship, she tends to get clingy and needy. She has also realized that this behavior turns her partners off. Still, she feels as though she just can't help herself. For example, one

day her previous boyfriend, Bob had, announced that he was going on a weekend cruise with his friends. Lisa knew that these cruises were like parties, with drinking and dancing, and she worried that he might "hook up" with another woman. As she thought about what might happen on the boat, she felt her breath quicken and her heart beat rapidly. She heard herself start to question him about what he was planning to do on the cruise. When he told her what he and his friends usually did, she felt even more uncertain. Her heart beat even faster and she started to sweat. Feeling panicky, she started seeking reassurances that Bob really did care about her. He became irritated and provided vague answers. His hesitancy prompted Lisa to feel even more scared and act even more clingy. The relationship ended two weeks later. Lisa notes that this pattern of insecurity leading to breakup has been pretty typical of her relationships.

In the episode described above, Lisa dealt with her negative feelings about Bob's going on a cruise by trying to get rid of them through seeking assurances from Bob. In ACT, this "seeking assurance" behavior would be seen as experiential avoidance. In the short term, Lisa's feelings of uncertainty might abate when she gets such assurance (in an example of negative reinforcement), but in the long run, she, in fact, pushes partners away. Here is an example of how an ACT therapist might help Lisa embrace feelings of fear and uncertainty through the cultivation of mindfulness and self-compassion.

Therapist: Lisa, I'm interested in that feeling when you start to become uncertain, just before you start "clinging." Would you be willing to bring that feeling into this room with me now and explore it? I think that this feeling may be something that is pulling you off track.

Lisa: I think you're right. This feeling of being unsure of myself has been around a long time. I wish I could get rid of it, once and for all! Yeah, we can explore it, but I can already hear myself looking for excuses not to have to feel it.

Therapist: That's exactly what I need to understand. If you would be willing to explore this with me, I think I would better understand and be better able to help you. If you really want to move on in your life, I think exploring this feeling is a way to do just that.

Lisa: Okay, I'm willing. I really want to stop being needy and move on. I just want to be with someone who loves me.

Therapist: Becoming intimate with others requires you to be intimate with yourself. Exploring this feeling you have in detail is a way to get in touch with what happens with you in these situations. So, go ahead, Lisa. See if you can connect with this feeling of uncertainty by imagining the last time it happened. The first thing we are going to do is just observe it.

Lisa: Okay, I'll go back to a scene the last week before Bob and I broke up. Oh, this is easy. I feel that awful feeling now. (Her breathing increases, her jaw muscles tighten, and her face becomes flushed.)

Therapist: (*noticing Lisa's reaction*) That's excellent, Lisa; I can see that you have gotten in touch with that feeling. See if it is possible to just explore it together with me. I don't want you to talk about the feeling; just feel it. Can you put your hand on the places on your body where you feel it? Start with where you feel it the most. Don't describe it; just feel it. Move your hand along your body from the place you feel it most to the other places you feel it. This will show me where you are feeling. You can circle the areas with your hand so I see how big they are.

(Lisa shows with her hand that the feeling starts in her stomach area and goes up to her chest and shoulders, then her jaws and head. She circles with her fingers the areas affected.)

Therapist: That's excellent, Lisa. Now let's just stay here. I want you to keep this feeling so that we can explore it. See if you can make the negative feelings stay. Imagine that these feelings are like your children, and I want you to embrace them together with me. Hold them, and breathe gently into them, and see if you can keep them still so that we can look even more closely.

(Lisa nods and puts her hands on the places she felt these feelings as if to embrace them and breathe gently into them. After a few minutes, she stops, surprised.)

Lisa: I'm sorry—I can't keep them. When I try to embrace them, they disappear. I can't hold on to them; they keep going away!

Therapist: Oh no—see if you can hang on to them. Maybe we can go on an anxiety hunt and find them. Can you feel them anywhere else in your body? Check and see!

(Lisa checks.)

Lisa: No, I am sorry—they're just gone. I can't get them back.

Therapist: Do you see what just happened, Lisa? What happened when you invited in your negative feelings of uncertainty—actually embracing and welcoming them?

Lisa: They ran the other way!

Therapist: What conclusion could you draw from this experience?

Lisa: Wow, is it really that simple? All these years of trying to get rid of that feeling, after all I've suffered—could it really be that simple?

Therapist: Every time you run away from a feeling, it looks bigger and more dangerous. But, actually, there are no feelings that you're not big enough to have. You're always greater than any feeling you might have. And any feeling, no matter how much you like or don't like it, will pass and change. If you approach feelings just as you did now, you'll see this. As soon as you sense a feeling that you're reacting to—that you're resisting—just stop. Put your hand on where you feel it and see if you can hold it like an infant. Give it oxygen by breathing into it. Give it space. You'll see that it will pass. But don't take my word for it. Try this yourself and collect some data!

In this example, by asking Lisa to "approach" a feeling that she has previously habitually avoided, the therapist is facilitating a process whereby the verbal (relational) network in which Lisa's anxiety participates is able to acquire new and different stimulus functions—more specifically, "approach" rather than "avoidance." From an RFT point of view, a key aspect of this is Lisa's self-as-process: the ongoing verbal discrimination of her psychological processes (e.g., feelings of anxiety). The therapist tries to establish different functions for certain of these processes (i.e., anxiety) by presenting new rules that prescribe acceptance rather than avoidance. Willingness to approach the unacceptable feeling is further encouraged through motivative augmental control—the RFT conceptualization of valuing—by adding ingredients of Lisa's valued direction of intimacy. Lisa experiences the true nature of this negative feeling. She experiences how her body reacts to this feeling. She pauses and tenderly touches herself, which stimulates her parasympathetic nervous system, has a calming effect, and breaks the vicious cycle of reacting adversely to her reactions. Embracing her feeling and her initial physical resistance is a powerful move in the direction of self-compassion and an alternative to the controlling behaviors that have pushed away her partners.

Observing Difficult and Judgmental Thoughts Without Entanglement

A second step in self-compassion involves noticing when one is being judgmental of oneself and one's actions. Under typical circumstances, not only do people react with physical resistance to difficult thoughts and feelings, but they also amplify their suffering by judging themselves negatively for having such feelings and reactions. Just as these difficult feelings are conditioned, so is judgmental behavior. An act of self-compassion would be to observe these judgments and show kindness and empathy in regard to them without further entanglement. This is the process of cognitive defusion. Remember that the purpose of defusion is to increase contact with the process of thinking and decrease the power of the products of thinking, or thoughts. We might characterize an act of self-compassion as a playful, flexible, and creative way of relating to these thoughts. Below, we describe how an ACT therapist might work with Lisa's entanglement with her thoughts.

Lisa has now made many attempts to embrace her difficult feelings by simply noticing the physical sensations, opening up to them, and breathing with them. She has found this very helpful and has become more intimate with the way these feelings influence her body. Further, she has noticed that certain thoughts almost always trigger these feelings and sensations. This week, she was asked to write down these thoughts and bring them to therapy. Here is the list Lisa brought.

+ *I am a phony.*

+ *Compared to these other people, I am much worse.*

+ *I have to really look good or be very successful in order to be accepted.*

+ *If he really got to know me, he would run the other way.*

Therapist: Did you notice, Lisa, that just the fact that you identified these thoughts and could write them down means that you separated the thinker from the thoughts? How did that feel?

Lisa: When I started writing them down, I felt ashamed because I know I am not supposed to have these thoughts, and then I had to laugh at myself for judging my own judging.

Therapist: What you just did there, Lisa, is exactly what I want to explore with you today. You not only looked at your thoughts, which means you were able to *see* your thoughts rather than *be* your thoughts, but you were able to laugh at how your mind works. You can see that the nature of the mind is to judge you pretty harshly. And that's the way it is for everyone, no matter how accomplished he or she is.

Lisa: So you mean all that judgment doesn't actually mean anything? Like bad self-confidence?

Therapist: Yes, exactly. The critical mind is a constant. Once you accept this, you can smile and be compassionate with it. You can see by your data collection that these thoughts had the power to pull you off course in those situations in which something was important to you.

Lisa: Yeah, they were situations where I wanted to get closer to someone, mostly. And I ended up further away and feeling bad about myself.

Therapist: That's what thoughts will do if you let them. The secret, Lisa, is that thoughts actually have no power over you unless you give them power.

Lisa: Wow, it'd be a relief not to be a slave to my negative thoughts. How do I do that?

Therapist: Let's do an exercise where you can experience a way to relate to your thoughts in a more compassionate, flexible manner. If you are willing, close your eyes and we can explore different ways of relating to your thoughts. By experimenting, you can see which ways are most helpful for you.

(Lisa nods and closes her eyes.)

Therapist: With your eyes closed, I want you just to notice your breathing. Just notice where you feel your breathing in your body. Feel the rhythm. See if you can just help your body by making room and allowing your body to do what it does best, which is to take care of you. See this as an act of self-compassion as you sit back, open up, and allow your body to breathe while coming into balance. Feel how your body knows exactly what to do, so that you just need to get out of the way and allow it to care for you. This is an act of self-compassion.

Now imagine that you are in a room that is white, bright with light, and empty, except for a single chair in the middle. This is your chair. It is not just a regular chair—more like a throne. The ceilings are high, and there are many windows and a door. I'd like to open the door and put a sign on the door that says "Open House." You know that an open house means that any guests are welcome—not just the people you invite, but anyone at all is welcome. Put up the sign, open the door, and sit in your throne. This throne makes you a little higher than your guests. I will place a pillow at your feet, and this is where you may invite your guests to sit and speak their mind. Your job is to see if you can treat each guest with compassion and respect, as you would treat children in your care, regardless of what their message is. See if you can notice how your body is reacting to each guest; feel your tendencies to act, but just sit calmly and make room for any reactions without acting on them.

Sit back and allow any guests who wish to come, in the form of thoughts, into your room. Ask them one at a time to sit at your feet, and ask them to speak. Be prepared for anything. Some of your guests will whine, and some may cry; some may be angry and others happy. While you maintain equanimity, notice your own reactions to the different thoughts and see if you also can be compassionate with your reactions to these guests. (Waits for several minutes, allowing Lisa to welcome her thoughts in such a way.) Lisa, let me invite you to return your attention to the room where you're here with me. Let me ask you, how did you experience this way of relating to your thoughts?

Lisa: I felt much more compassionate toward them, even though I felt myself reacting strongly to some. I even felt compassionate toward my own reactions. I know I have a history of reacting in this way that shuts me off from feelings, and I could understand that this type of shutting down was just a way I tried to protect myself from being hurt. It was an old habit that meant well but isn't helpful any longer.

Therapist: Wow, that's quite an insight. This is what we want to do: be clear-sighted about which thoughts and reactions are helpful and which are not. If a habit, like this "shutting down," is not helpful in moving toward intimacy, then regarding it compassionately rather than judging it harshly might be a way you can help yourself move forward. This coming week, see if you can use this experience as a way of identifying reactions and thoughts that are not so helpful, and see if you can untangle yourself from them by doing what you just did. Look at

> them from your throne and know that you
> *have* these thoughts—but that you *are not*
> these thoughts—and see if you can treat both
> the passing thoughts and subsequent reactions
> with compassion. Gather some data, and see if
> this compassionate way of relating to your
> inner life is helpful to you.

From an RFT point of view, the step just presented (i.e., observing difficult and judgmental thoughts) is similar to the previous step (i.e., embracing difficult feelings) in that, once again, an attempt is made to establish a different set of functions for a potentially problematic type of behavior. In this step, however, the behavior concerned is more explicitly and exclusively a type of verbal behavior (i.e., relational framing). Further, because verbal behavior is such a strongly established, pervasive, and powerful repertoire (and indeed the core process involved in problematic fusion), it may be more difficult for some clients to discriminate it as separate from themselves in order to allow defusion and mitigation of the typical transformation of functions through the relational network. In Lisa's case, the therapist attempts to facilitate defusion by presenting, through metaphor, hierarchical relational network in which Lisa's self (self-as-context) is higher than and able to observe particular thoughts that have been or are currently being derived. The aim is to support a context that enables these thoughts to be hierarchically framed as THERE and THEN within Lisa's behavioral repertoire, as opposed to operating as an unnoticeable aspect of her current behavior HERE and NOW and, in this way, facilitate defusion from them.

Connecting with a More Spiritual Sense of Self

A third step in self-compassionate behavior entails getting into contact with a transcendent sense of self. It involves experiencing a self that is "larger" than how people typically experience themselves and the world. Using perspective-taking exercises, clients can look back at themselves from a wiser future. The idea is to help them distinguish between the content of consciousness and the self as a perspective-taking context for that content. In addition to loosening the tendency toward dualism, this helps reduce attachment to the conceptualized self. Here is how an ACT therapist might have Lisa do one such relatively simple exercise.

> *Therapist:* Lisa, can you create and feel that feeling of vulnerability and shutting down right now? Would you be willing to bring it here, right now?
>
> *Lisa:* Yeah, it's never far off. I can just think of the last time it happened. Yeah, I feel it now.
>
> *Therapist:* Okay, let's try this. Shut your eyes and see if you can just relax and see what kinds of pictures pop up that you associate with this feeling. See if you maybe can find the first time you noticed the experience of shutting down in this way.
>
> *Lisa:* (*shuts eyes*) Okay, I do have a picture. Should I tell you what is happening?
>
> *(Therapist nods.)*

Lisa: In this picture, I am seven years old. I had just gotten my first report card from school and had hurried home to show it to my parents. But as I came in the door, I heard them in a drunken fight and started to feel queasy. I peeked into the kitchen, where they were red-faced and yelling at each other. That's when I shut down and went to my room.

Therapist: This really helps me understand how this shutting down evolved. When you see that little seven-year-old girl scared and shutting down, how do you feel toward her?

Lisa: Loving—and sad that she had to go through that.

Therapist: Let's do an exercise where you write to this seven-year-old Lisa from your perspective here and now. I would like you to communicate with her in a love letter. How do you feel about her shutting down here?

(Lisa takes a few minutes and writes a brief note.)

Lisa: *(reading aloud)* Dear Little Lisa: You were right to want to show your parents your report card. You had done well in school, and you were proud to show them the nice things your teacher had written about your progress in school. Because your parents were so focused on their own problems, they weren't able to give you that attention that you deserved. It wasn't your fault, little Lisa. You are perfect just the way you are. When you gave up on them and went to your room, you did exactly right. You took care of yourself in the only way you could have in that moment. I am proud of you for doing what you had to do.

Therapist: How did that feel? How do you feel toward little Lisa and toward yourself writing to her?

Lisa: Feels very good. (*Her eyes fill with tears.*) I guess, before, I was judging her very harshly, but now I can see that she did the best she could. I feel a lot of love for her!

Therapist: So you can see that the shutting down was helpful for little Lisa and that's how that habit got going, and today that same shutting down is not so helpful in situations where you, here and now, want to move toward intimacy. Would it be possible for you to take this position of the compassionate observer when it happens to you now? Make room for this "little Lisa" reaction and then go forward? Just know where it comes from and be patient with it.

Writing a love letter to herself involves Lisa *here and now* taking perspective on Lisa there and then. More often than not, people look directly from the "I THERE and THEN" perspective, and can be harsh and judgmental with themselves. Writing from "I HERE and NOW" to "YOU THERE and THEN" (their past self as another person) helps clients see that their behavior was formed by that particular context; and this makes it easier for them to accept and forgive themselves. This kind of perspective-taking skill can be very helpful in getting clients "unstuck" from self-destructive behavior patterns.

An RFT interpretation of what is happening in the dialogue above is that Lisa is once again taking a "self-as-context" perspective, which undermines the typical transformation of functions that occurs when one relationally frames about things or people in the world, including himself or herself (e.g., "I am a failure") or even his or her own relational framing (e.g., "I just had the thought *I am a failure*; how typical of me to think self-negating thoughts like that"). This time, however, the "self-as-context" metaphor is supplemented by a metaphor of compassionate action that supports a particular pattern of transformation of functions. The therapist presents a relational network in which Lisa (present Lisa) can respond to her past self (little Lisa) as if to another person (i.e., as YOU THERE and THEN). Her doing so changes the context of her thoughts and feelings in a very particular way, one that not only shows them to be part of her behavior but also supports empathic responding with regard to that behavior. Similar to other relational networks brought to bear with respect to behavior, this undermines defusion; in addition, it brings an important additional empathic quality to the transformation of functions.

Compassionate Engagement in Self-Validation

The final aspect of self-compassionate behavior involves acting in ways that matter. Not acting in ways that matter—going through life aimlessly, disconnected from what matters to one personally—is, we suggest, actually a form of violence and cruelty to one's self, since it denies what is needed for one's own psychological health and thus causes needless psychological harm and suffering. On the other hand, to engage in stimulating, vital activities—those that provide one with a sense of meaningfulness while helping him or her become stronger and more flexible—is an act of self-compassion. These activities might provide restoration, stimulate creativity, or just help one make contact with the natural contingencies of life, which can be intrinsically reinforcing. One way of promoting compassionate engagement in self-validation is to work with the Values Compass (see, e.g., Hayes et al. 1999; see also chapter 7). The purpose of the Values Compass is to help clients clearly define what matters to them, create a sense of meaning and purpose, provide a context in which they may be more willing to experience difficult thoughts and feelings, and help them become more aware of the reinforcing qualities of behaviors in the moment that are related to a larger value.

Self-compassion may be considered to underlie all values. This means that taking care of oneself in a long-term healthy fashion is an overarching valued direction. From that perspective, clients can explore their values in a variety of life domains. In the Values Compass, intimacy is only one of ten domains. Metaphorically, these domains are similar to the spokes on a bicycle wheel. The more healthy and vital these spokes are, the more balanced the ride is.

In the Values Compass exercise, clients are asked to describe in a few words what they think might be the essence of their value in each domain. The ACT therapist would suggest that clients imagine self-compassion as the underpinning value of each domain, which means looking at each domain from a perspective that considers what is best for them in the long term. Clients are also asked to focus on lifelong values rather than on their goals in the present situation, and to identify the function or reinforcing qualities of each of those values (the therapist might support the latter process as needed). Below is an example of a completed Values Compass exercise that includes the reinforcing qualities that appear to characterize each domain.

Domain	Lifelong value	Function/ reinforcing qualities
1. Work	With my special talents and capabilities, I want to contribute to work life in a meaningful way.	I can feel connected to the whole by contributing to the good of the whole community in whatever way possible.
2. Leisure	I want to give myself time every day to develop my own special interests. I like to paint and write.	We all have special talents and interests that may vary over our lifetime. Ideally, we would allow ourselves time, space, and resources to develop these special talents regardless of our conditions, and in whatever form they may take.
3. Caregiving	I want to give myself time to nourish and take care of someone or some living thing regularly in my life. In that relationship, I want to be present and dependable. Right now, I would like to volunteer at the public school.	Taking care of someone or some living thing appears to have a unique, reinforcing quality and a positive effect on health and well-being.

4. Family	Giving and receiving emotional and practical support. I want to have regular contact with my parents and siblings and help them when I am able.	I can receive unconditional acceptance; I will have a supportive community; my family and I will celebrate milestones and transitions in life together.
5. Intimate relations	I want to be in a relationship in which physical and emotional closeness are part of my daily routine. I want to be open and honest with my partner, accepting him/her for who he/she is and feeling accepted as well.	I will benefit from the physical touch, sexual enjoyment, emotional intimacy, and acceptance that intimate relations afford.
6. Community involvement	I want to actively participate in the community that I live in and share a sense of responsibility for those around me. Right now that means sorting recyclables from garbage every day.	Being connected to a community in common efforts for the good of the whole community
7. Spirituality	I want to give myself time every day to reflect on my life and what I am doing. Right now, I would like to practice mindfulness 15 minutes a day.	I can experience a connection with nature and fellow human beingsI will also learn to be still and open up so as to better accept private events

Domain	Lifelong value	Function/ reinforcing qualities
8. Education and personal development	I want to keep myself open to the challenge of learning new things every day. Right now, I would like to learn Spanish.	Learning something new helps us develop as human beings. Being open to and curious regarding new experiences facilitates activity in this domain.
9. Health	Every time I eat, I want to be aware that I am nourishing my body and giving it what it needs, including the right amount of sleep and exercise. Right now, I want to take a 30-minute walk after work and make a proper meal every night.	Mindfully taking care of our own physical needs (nutrition needs, hygiene, sleep, and exercise) can be experienced as vital.
10. Social network	Having a small group of friends in which I feel accepted and accepting, feel open and honest, and have a sense of belonging. Right now, I could arrange to have dinner with a group of people from work.	I will be able to benefit from feeling connected to a group of people outside of family; experiencing life's activities, process, and transitions together with others, and feeling accepted and supported.

Functions of Values Domains

One of the important features of the values domains listed in the Values Compass is to demonstrate that, particular reinforcing qualities or psychological functions stay constant for everyone. In other words, values like "belonging to a group" persist throughout one's life regardless of changes in living situation, relationship status, and other variables. The reinforcing quality of being touched may be functionally the same in old age as it was in infancy. In the same way, the reinforcing quality of developing one's own talents and interests may be no different in terms of function whether one lives in a prison or a castle. Friendships, exercise, and time taken to develop one's own interests may be no less important when one is "madly in love" or when one has young children than at any other time. Unfortunately, many people neglect these other domains and obsessively focus on the intimate relations domain alone. Cutting off important sources of positive reinforcement creates a vulnerability, like "putting all your eggs in one basket." As we discussed in chapter 7, it is important to maintain variety across values domains, which can promote the healthy functioning of intimate relationships.

You might consider doing this exercise yourself. As you consider your values in these ten domains, see whether you can go beyond the "programmed" answers usually expressed in our culture. Step away from the content of your values and think about them from a functional perspective. For example, in the work domain, the satisfaction of doing your best and getting the job done has probably been qualitatively the same, from the first job you had in your youth right up to the job you have now. The reinforcing qualities or meaning of each domain is probably fairly consistent, transcending changes in actual content throughout your life. Think about the qualities of your friendships. Can you see an overarching quality in friendships you value, no matter your age or life situation?

Here is how an ACT therapist might work with Lisa using the Values Compass she completed.

> *Therapist:* Hi, Lisa. Let's take a look at the Values Compass you did. I see that you identified your values in each area. Let's use the compass and see if it helps you see the parts of your life that are being neglected.

> *Lisa:* I already noticed. I see that I don't have balance.

> *Therapist:* Good that you can see that. But let's take a look. As you look at each of these ten areas, give each one a number from one to ten to show how important that area is in your life. I am not asking if you are active in that area at the moment, but rather just if you think it is an important area. A "one" would show that it is not important, while a "ten" shows that it is very important. Don't compare the areas. All the areas can be given a ten, and don't think about how much you're expressing these values currently. This is a general question: Is this an important area in your life?

> *(Lisa writes all eights, nines, and tens on her compass.)*

> *Therapist:* That's great, Lisa—you really know that all of these aspects of life are important.

> *(Lisa nods.)*

Therapist: The next part is different. I want you to rate your own behavior in each area. Think of how active you have been in creating that quality you want in each aspect over the past two weeks. For example, you have written: "I want to be in a relationship where physical and emotional closeness are part of my daily routine. I want to be open and honest with my partner, accepting him/her for who he/she is and feeling accepted as well." For you, the rewarding qualities in this area include physical touch, sexual enjoyment, emotional intimacy, and acceptance. The question is then, on a scale of zero to ten, how active have you been in creating emotional and physical closeness with your partner in the past two weeks?

Lisa reveals that she has not been particularly active in intimate relations (1), family (0), social network (0), caregiving (0), or community involvement (0). Her ratings for other areas are also low: health (2), spirituality (0), and leisure (0). Only in two areas, namely, work (10) and education and personal development (7), are her ratings high. It is clear to Lisa that she has been neglecting her own needs as well as her relationships—intimate and otherwise. This exercise helps her see the discrepancy between what she knows is important to her and how she has been investing her time and energy. Seeing this discrepancy is motivating for Lisa—it makes her want to start working on putting her life back in balance. The compass exercise also helps her see function over form. For example, the long-term and overarching values she has contacted with regard to intimate relationships have no particular form—that is, they are not dependent on the gender of the partner whom she chooses.

Functions of Behavior

Once a client has made contact with long-term and over-arching valued directions, the next step is to investigate the function of behavior that might affect movement in those valued directions. People's behavior affects their proclaimed values. One of the aims of ACT is to help clients become conscious of the function of their chosen patterns of behavior, especially with respect to their values. Are clients' particular patterns of behavior congruent with their proclaimed values, or do they block or prevent pursuit of those values? A key question for clients to ask themselves when they are engaging in an activity is "What is this activity in the service of?"

As you probably already know, many everyday activities are done out of habit rather than because of deliberate choice. Habits can be counter to values. For example, when you get home from work, you might automatically flop down on the couch and turn on the TV. If you value exercise and aim to get thirty minutes of exercise every day, this behavior of flopping down in front of the TV is not congruent with your values in the way that going for a jog would be.

Other activities might be deliberately chosen as steps in a valued direction, but as they become routine, their connection to values may be lost. Imagine that a man chooses to visit his elderly mother each day on his way home from work, thus taking a step consistent with his valued direction in the domain of family. The function starts off being values-congruent. However, as time passes, this same activity starts feeling like a chore, and the man visits more out of a sense of obligation than as a step in valued living. In this way, the function of the behavior becomes avoidance of a bad conscience.

The Values Compass exercise can help people see whether the functions of particular patterns of behavior are values-congruent. The Values Compass may reveal discrepancies between what people say they value and how they are actually behaving. For example, Barry may say that he values friendships, but since he has been in his current relationship, he has neglected his friends. Barry's recent neglect of his friendships does not *change* his stated value; it is simply incongruent. This fact would show up as he did the Values Compass exercise, because there would be a discrepancy between his ratings of the importance of the social network domain and his actual behavior in this domain over the past two weeks. Identifying the overarching value in a particular domain and then examining inconsistencies in behavior in this way usually motivates behavior change.

The RFT interpretation of this process is similar to the consideration of values as augmental control described in previous chapters (e.g., chapter 7). From this perspective, as with any form of behavior that one may wish to encourage, an ACT therapist might make patterns of action on the part of a client that coordinate with self-compassion more likely by relating them to particular values. The restatement of behavior as being related to values thus increases the likelihood that the behavior will be reinforcing.

Summary

Self-compassion provides a foundation for long-term loving intimacy with others. The basic steps in self-compassion involve becoming aware of one's own conditioned reactions that pull one away from intimate behavior, learning to make room for and embrace these reactions, noticing thoughts and feelings without amplifying them, and engaging in meaningful actions that are validating. In particular, the Values Compass provides a way to explore values across multiple domains, thus providing a basis for healthier relationships and psychological flexibility. In the next chapter, we explore what happens when love goes awry and couples seek psychotherapy.

CHAPTER 9

Couples Therapy

Introduction

One of the themes of this book has been that the romantic ideal of love gives rise to problems. We have explained the emergence and perpetuation of relationship problems from the perspectives of behavior analysis, RFT, and ACT. A key purpose of this chapter is to examine therapy for relationships, from an ACT/RFT perspective as well as the perspectives of a number of dedicated forms of couples therapy. To start with, we present a case study of a relationship in difficulty, followed by an ACT/RFT conceptualization of this case. We then introduce and review research on a number of forms of couples therapy, and subsequently examine how these approaches might consider the case study, in comparison with ACT. These treatments for couples clearly differ from ACT; nevertheless, there are areas of overlap. Furthermore, one of the key advantages of ACT is that it meshes well with RFT's analysis of complex human behavior, which facilitates the practical understanding in terms of more basic processes not just of ACT but also of other approaches. Hence, in our analysis we also examine these forms of couples therapy through the lens of RFT, explaining some of the phenomena and interventions from this perspective. In this way, we elucidate how recent developments in couples therapy are consistent with ACT and RFT.

Case Study: Jonas and Eva

Jonas had always had trouble with dating. Since he was a little boy, he found himself feeling nervous and shy around girls, especially in social situations. He avoided talking to them in the lunchroom or on the playground. Later, as a teenager, he never participated in after-school activities. He began to think of himself as "shy," "awkward," and "a loser." When he was in class, though, it was a different story. He generally did well in school, and consequently he did not feel stressed when the focus was on academics. In these situations, he came across as confident and self-assured. Even with female students, when conversations revolved around schoolwork—his specialty—Jonas did not feel scared or uncomfortable. However, as soon as class ended, he returned to feeling out of sorts, telling himself that he was "unable to connect" with women.

This same pattern continued in college. Early in his freshman year, some friends invited him to a party. Even though he felt nervous, he went along, steeling his nerves by drinking alcohol. Initially, he had a lot of fun dancing with different women. However, as the night wore on, he got so drunk that he vomited at the party. Later, when his friends distributed photos of him dancing (and vomiting) via social media, he felt ridiculed and ashamed. He decided that he "looked like an idiot" and that parties were "not [his] thing." As a result, he recommitted himself to his academic work, graduating *summa cum laude*.

After graduation, he began working in the financial services industry. At a company picnic, he met Eva, one of his coworkers. Eva was a very outgoing person, and she initially approached Jonas "because he looked cute." She found him very interesting and introspective, which she appreciated, having dated many "narcissistic jerks" in the past. Eva pursued a relationship with Jonas vigorously. When accompanied by Eva, Jonas was more comfortable going out socially; he no longer felt like a "social misfit."

Initially, for Jonas, going out with Eva was fun and improved his life. Eva appreciated that she and Jonas could have long, intimate discussions over dinner in quiet, romantic settings or snuggle up in front of the television in the evening. With the excitement, the sexual energy, and all the other goodies of new love and romance, it felt to Jonas and Eva that they had found a great balance—that they "completed" each other. After a couple years of dating, they got married and had a baby girl.

At this point, however, problems started to emerge in their relationship. Jonas no longer enjoyed going out, preferring to stay at home. Meanwhile, Eva did not tolerate staying at home very well. She tried to ensure that they went out as a couple regularly enough, even as Jonas displayed increasing lack of enthusiasm for socializing. When they did go out, Jonas relied on Eva to provide safety in social situations. However, Eva became irritated with the way he would cling to her whenever they were out with friends. At parties she would whisper to him, "It is your responsibility to mingle, and I don't want you always hanging on me." He began to assert his desire to stay home and not go out. Usually by Wednesday night each week, they would be arguing about the coming weekend. Jonas resented Eva for "pressuring" him to do what felt increasingly uncomfortable. Eva, on the other hand, felt miserably bored staying at home. She wanted to spend time with Jonas, but she bristled against spending multiple weekends watching television or playing a board game. Whenever they could get a babysitter, she insisted that they take advantage and go out. Over the years, numerous interactions like this contributed to Jonas and Eva becoming intolerant of each other and unable to discuss the issue without fighting.

When they come for treatment, Eva complains of feeling "bored" and "stagnant" in the relationship, and she worries that they are drifting apart. She accuses Jonas of being "a stick in the mud" who does his best to ensure that they never go out and have fun. Although she loves spending time with Jonas and their daughter, she also craves more social interaction. When she has to go to parties alone, she feels disappointed and resentful. As for Jonas, he says angrily, "There's no time for just the two of us anymore." He describes their busy professional lives and expresses a strong desire to simply relax at home with his family. He bitterly calls Eva a "party animal" who needs to accept the reality of their domestic life. He admits to feeling anxious in most social settings, noting dejectedly that he is "not a people person." Although he does enjoy going to happy hour with coworkers occasionally, he often finds himself feeling too tired to go out.

An ACT/RFT Perspective

In chapter 5, we pointed out that language has provided much richness and good for the human species, and that language also causes a great deal of suffering not seen in other members of the animal kingdom. Because people do not just live in the moment at hand, but also interact verbally with their own learning histories, these histories come to play a role in intimate relationships. Couples can become fused with statements about how things should be (i.e., rules and stereotypes). For example, Jonas sees himself ("self-as-content") as shy and socially withdrawn. Whenever Eva encourages him to join in at a party, or to go out dancing, he responds to self-as-content and to a learning history that includes moments of public embarrassment.

Jonas was initially attracted to Eva because she was outgoing, while she found his shyness and introspection endearing. It is not uncommon for people to seek out a partner who can add to their life things that they have difficulty adding on their own. This is not necessarily problematic, but as we have stated earlier, when the function of a relationship, or motivation to seek an intimate partner, is to make up for a perceived deficit, fusion with self-as-content can be problematic. So, if Jonas was initially attracted to Eva because he wanted to be with someone who would improve his social life, this could be problematic.

Certainly people can try to find a balance; for example, knowing that you are not likely to engage in social activities and finding a partner who will be more likely to organize social outings could lead to meaningful encounters. However, if Jonas expects Eva to compensate for his shyness, this can keep him fused with self-as-content. Jonas may also be fused with statements about Eva, expecting her to always follow a stereotype of being a "social butterfly." In this respect, he (or Eva) could be stuck in thinking about other-as-content.

Problems can develop when one or both partners develop an expectation that the other will always act in a certain fashion. Briefly, if Jonas is fused with the statement "Eva is a social butterfly" but finds that, once they start a family, she begins to enjoy being home with the children more, he may feel disappointment that she is not compensating for his deficits any longer. Or if Eva is fused with the statement "Jonas is shy and introverted," but notices that after they attend a variety of social situations together, Jonas begins to seek social interactions, mingle freely at parties, and develop his own group of friends, she may experience distress that he no longer needs her and fear that they don't have the same deep connection they once had. In this situation, polarization (Jacobson & Christensen, 1998) occurs, because Jonas and Eva are acting on rigid rules for each other's behavior. When either of them behaves in a flexible fashion—Eva enjoying quiet time with the kids at home, or Jonas going out for a beer with his buddies—there is conflict. As their need to avoid discomfort (see chapter 6) increases, they begin to argue increasingly, trying to force the other to "act like he/she should." They get stuck in a frantic search for "happiness," which they've defined as a relationship without conflict, one in which they always meet each other's expectations.

Now let us examine several forms of dedicated couples therapy and how they might conceptualize this case study in comparison to an ACT/RFT perspective.

Forms of Couples Therapy

There are many forms of couples therapy. The theoretical backdrop of this book, however, is behavioral. Therefore we limit our discussion of couples therapies that have empirical support to those that have arisen from the behavioral or cognitive behavioral tradition. Generally speaking, distressed couples who participate in some form of therapy are better off than those who do not seek treatment (Shadish & Baldwin, 2003). In addition, certain forms of couples therapy have been shown to be particularly efficacious. In a meta-analysis conducted by Shadish and Baldwin (2003), for example, couples receiving behavioral therapy demonstrated significant improvement across a variety of measures compared to couples who did not receive therapy. A follow-up analysis, which included unpublished doctoral dissertations, substantiated the helpfulness of behavioral therapy for couples (Shadish & Baldwin, 2005).

There are four major behavioral psychotherapies for couples: behavioral therapy (also referred to as "traditional behavioral couples therapy," or TBCT, in the literature), cognitive behavioral therapy (CBT), enhanced CBT (ECBT), and integrative behavioral couples therapy (IBCT). Traditional behavioral couples therapy laid the groundwork in the field by focusing on the development of specific skills in each partner. The subsequent couples therapies built upon this approach, retaining its behavioral emphasis and adding other dimensions.

Traditional Behavioral Couples Therapy

Traditional behavioral couples therapy (TBCT; Jacobson & Margolin, 1979) comprises training in behavior exchange, communication skills, and problem solving. Behavior exchange addresses the common relationship issue that partners would like to see each other commit to specific behavioral changes. By each creating a list of desired changes in the other's behavior, partners are able to negotiate for what they would like, while selectively agreeing to act on the other's requests, too. The formula is pretty straightforward; it's akin to saying, "If you do this for me, then I'll do this for you." Communication skills taught in TBCT are particularly helpful when couples are prone to conflict and arguments. Each partner is taught how to express feelings, needs, and wants in ways that are more readily heard and understood by the other. In addition, each is guided in how to listen to the other. The most common example of a technique taught in communication training is the use of "I-statements": each partner is advised to talk about himself or herself, as opposed to the other person (i.e., avoid "You-statements"). This simple intervention can reduce partners' defensiveness and promote effective communication. In this way, it paves the way for problem solving in which partners learn how to brainstorm together and distinguish solution-focused conversations from emotional ones.

Meta-analyses done in the 1980s and early 1990s of traditional behavioral couples therapy suggest that couples do improve following treatment (e.g., Jacobson et al., 1984; Shadish et al., 1993). Christensen and Heavey (1999) reported that studies during this time concluded that 36.1 percent to 41 percent of couples showed reliable improvement in both partners, with therapy bringing the partners from a level of distress to non-distress.

Cognitive Behavioral Couples Therapy

Cognitive behavioral couples therapy includes the same components as behavioral couples therapy, with an additional focus on cognitive restructuring of dysfunctional beliefs. Couples are taught about the dangers of automatic thinking, such as mind reading and overgeneralization. Then, they learn how to assess the accuracy of their thoughts, perhaps by asking each other non-blaming questions related to a particular situation. Suppose, for example, that one partner is late in meeting the other. The one who is on time might think *He doesn't care about me* or *I'm always number 2 in his life.* Through cognitive restructuring, this partner would question this negative thinking and inquire directly with the other about his or her tardiness. Cognitive behavioral couples therapy is often classified as "behavioral couples therapy" in meta-analyses and other studies; thus its effectiveness is comparable to TBCT. For example, Snyder, Castellani, and Whisman (2006) include "cognitive restructuring" as one of the components of behavioral couples therapy. In an effort to disentangle various behavioral couples therapies, Wood, Crane, Schaalje, and Law (2005) conducted a meta-analysis to look at effect sizes for (a) behavioral marital therapies, (b) cognitive behavioral marital therapies and other "mixed" therapies, and (c) therapies that contained only certain components of behavioral marital therapies. There were not significant differences between behavioral and cognitive behavioral couples therapies. However, the authors suggest that "treatment for moderately distressed couples should have a clear treatment plan that is followed" (p. 284), because the treatments that included only components of behavioral therapies, as opposed to being planned behavioral or cognitive behavioral interventions, had substantially lower gains than those treatments that followed a particular model and plan. Thus, it is important to use a clear conceptual framework, such as a cognitive behavioral perspective, when providing couples therapy.

Enhanced Cognitive Behavioral Couples Therapy

Epstein and Baucom (2002) have noted the impact of emotion focused therapy in the couples therapy literature and have suggested an "enhanced" cognitive behavioral couples therapy (ECBT), the objective of which is "to identify individuals' needs and personal goals at the same time as it improve[s] how individuals function as a team" (p. 21). Epstein and Baucom also suggest the need for therapists to attend to the individuals' motivations that comprise "cognitive schemas, emotional arousal and behavioral repertoires for meeting particular goals" (p. 109). The authors view a focus on motivation, conceptualized in this manner, as consistent with cognitive behavioral couples therapy. Thus, ECBT utilizes all the strategies of traditional behavior therapy when appropriate, attends to faulty assumptions and beliefs, and also addresses the impact of emotion on behavior and thinking. As with integrated cognitive behavior couples therapy (IBCT; see below), there is greater acknowledgment that each member of a couple has a unique history, a set of emotional responses to life, and schemas about the world and relationships. The therapy is "enhanced" in that therapists are now looking at all of these areas, and working within the CBT framework from conceptualization through treatment. The ECBT model "highlights the roles of demands, personal needs, environmental influences, and developmental changes" (Epstein & Baucom, 2002, p. 206) in a way that standard CBT for couples does not.

Integrative Behavioral Couples Therapy

A well-articulated model of couples therapy that combines behavioral therapy with emotion focused treatment is integrative behavioral couples therapy (IBCT; Jacobson & Christensen, 1998). IBCT was initially developed to help high-conflict couples for whom change was not necessarily forthcoming. As such, IBCT added components of acceptance and tolerance while working with couples at a more thematic level. In IBCT, couples are encouraged, with the help of the therapist, to develop understanding of how their relationship works. Once they have identified the dynamics of their relationship, couples have a novel context in which to experience its positive and negative aspects. For example, with IBCT, couples often realize that the source of their initial attraction can become problematic, depending on the circumstances. A partner who was desirable for being "laid-back" can quickly become demonized for being "lazy," even though the behavior is similar across different situations.

In the initial treatment outcome study comparing IBCT with TBCT, Christensen and colleagues (2004) found that both treatments resulted in clinically significant improvement, but more consistent improvement throughout treatment was noted for those couples who received IBCT. At two-year follow-up, 69 percent of IBCT couples were improved, compared to 60 percent of TBCT couples (Christensen et al., 2006). Half of the couples in both conditions showed an increase in relationship satisfaction after five years, with a slight advantage noted for IBCT (Christensen, Atkins, Baucom, & Yi, 2010).

We have now presented several forms of therapy used with couples. These approaches are theoretically related to each other, and thus they share certain features. At the same time, they are theoretically distinct, and thus each brings a somewhat different conceptualization and particular components to bear. In order to shed further light on the nature of these approaches, in what follows we examine how they might conceptualize Jonas and Eva's relationship, presented earlier. This also allows further opportunity for us to explore the differences between these approaches and ACT/RFT. ACT/RFT is uniquely advantaged in that RFT, which articulates relatively closely with ACT, enables a technical analysis of the processes involved in any theory (including ACT, as well as other therapies), which thus allows a useful level of comparison and contrast among different theoretical orientations. None of the couples therapies was developed coherent with an approach like RFT. However, several of the interventions used in these treatments can be explained, at least partially, by RFT. In the case conceptualizations that follow, therefore, we examine not only how particular approaches might interpret the case of Jonas and Eva, but also how RFT might interpret processes or techniques involved in these approaches.

Perspectives on Jonas and Eva

In what follows, we examine how the case of Jonas and Eva might be conceptualized and treated within each of the preceding approaches. Following each perspective is a section interpreting the approach from an ACT/RFT perspective.

A Traditional Behavioral Therapy Perspective

In traditional behavioral couples therapy (TBCT), the therapist is very active and directive in teaching specific skills. Let's look at how a traditional behavioral couples therapist would work with Jonas and Eva. Initially, the therapist would work to establish a collaborative set with the couple. With very distressed and polarized couples, each member of the couple collaborates not only with the other but also with the therapist. Each partner commits to the therapist to follow prescribed homework assignments. In this way, the therapist can circumvent the inevitable resistance to doing more work when partners blame each other for their problems. The earliest interventions are meant to increase the number of pleasant interactions the couple share by using behavior exchange exercises, whereby each member of the couple agrees to do small activities that the other would enjoy. When each member of the couple is engaging in these brief niceties, either on a daily basis or during a designated "love day" or other time period, both are getting some of the reinforcers they may have been wanting. As the couple's collaboration increases, and as their interactions improve during the behavior exchange exercises, the therapist

229

introduces training in communication skills and problem solving. In session, the partners practice stating behaviorally what the other may do that is distressing while avoiding statements that vilify him or her. They practice not interrupting, and they practice paraphrasing what the other has said in order to slow down the communication process, really hear each other out, and clarify any misunderstandings. Once they are able to communicate in this way, they begin to discuss particular problems, evaluate solutions, and agree on a plan of action. While TBCT is indeed an example of a mechanistic treatment (see chapter 2), data have proved that it helps many couples, and we should not underestimate how robust this treatment can be. However, it is limited. Koerner, Jacobson, and Christensen (1994) point out that "traditional change strategies are difficult to use with very distressed couples...and don't take into account differences that generate conflict but are relatively unchangeable" (p. 113).

Behavior Exchange: An ACT/RFT View

Within couples therapy, behavior exchange is a very powerful technique, especially when done sensitively to the wants of the receiver and willingness of the initiator. Ultimately, it is important that each partner contact the contingencies associated with engaging in a particular behavior (or receiving it), rather than relating to it solely through verbal means. In a word, the context in which the behavior exchange occurs is very important. For example, suppose Eva really wanted Jonas to take her dancing. Her motivation might be based on prior experiences in which she had a lot of fun with him when they went out. From an ACT perspective, this would be a helpful basis for making such a request. Alternatively, she might want him to take her dancing "because it would be good for him." In this latter instance, she is relating to behavior under the control of a rule, and attempting to bring Jonas's behavior under the control of this rule as well. If she makes her request based on this rule, Jonas is likely to resist; that is, he could argue as to whether going dancing was "good" for him or not. In addition, if Eva continues to relate to her request in this way, then, even assuming they did go dancing, she is less likely to enjoy the experience because she would continue to relate to his behavior through relational framing. For example, she might watch Jonas closely in order to judge the degree to which he was enjoying the experience. Furthermore, Jonas is unlikely to be happy being subject to her scrutiny in this way, and thus the likelihood of his enjoying himself would also be reduced.

Alternatively, suppose that—as part of a behavior exchange collaboratively set in session—Jonas decided to take Eva dancing. His verbally ascribed motivation is important to note. If he is curious about taking her to a particular place, then he might be more likely to contact the contingencies associated with dancing there. However, if after the session, he begins to think that taking Eva dancing is something that he "should" do, then it takes the form of a rule. Relating to the actual experience through these verbal relations could make it difficult to enjoy the experience or find more grounding meaning in it, even if it was openly and voluntarily agreed upon in session. Later, Jonas might relate to the behavior as "following orders" or "doing therapy homework," reducing his motivation over the long term.

Finally, the fundamental nature of behavior exchanges can be problematic. By establishing a rule akin to "I'll do this for you, if you do that for me," members of a couple run the risk of relating to each other only through this rule. For example, Jonas might take Eva dancing in order to enjoy seeing her enthusiasm and joy on the dance floor. This would likely be reinforcing for him. Alternatively, he might take her dancing with the expectation that she will "owe" him something. He would be less engaged in the experience, and he might even be belligerent. If he voices his expectation that Eva now must do something for him, the experience is likely to be aversive for both of them.

In these situations, we can see how a dominance of verbal relations during the process of behavior exchange can preclude contact with naturally reinforcing contingencies. Thus, in order to use behavior exchange effectively, an ACT therapist would pay exquisite attention to the language that partners use to describe their experience of the intervention. Thus, the focus is not simply on the behavior exchanged, but also on what each partner tells himself or herself about it.

Another element of TBCT mentioned earlier was communication training. One of the techniques taught in communication training is an emphasis on the use of "I-statements": statements beginning with "I" (statements about oneself), rather than "You." As suggested earlier, this is a method of reducing defensiveness in the other person and promoting effective communication.

From an RFT point of view, the focus on the deictic relational cues "I" and "You" is potentially significant for a number of reasons. First, because there is often the potential for the listener to interpret a "You-statement" as incongruent with his or her experience of the situation, a higher rate of such statements might make it more likely that the listener will derive that the speaker "doesn't understand me" and that, therefore, what the speaker is saying has little validity. Avoiding using "You-statements" may, therefore, be helpful in this respect. Another reason it may be helpful is that verbalization regarding the use of "I" and "You" might make both partners more mindful of their use of language, particularly with respect to declarations concerning the other person. In addition, use of "I" as opposed to "You" might, under some circumstances, help increase mindful awareness of self and values on the part of the speaker.

A Cognitive Behavioral Therapy (CBT) Perspective

A cognitive behavioral therapist might make use of communication training and teach problem solving as well, but he or she would also emphasize Eva's and Jonas's perceptions and rigid belief systems that cause them distress. A hallmark of CBT is cognitive restructuring, in which a client changes his or her belief about something in order to reflect a more objective, rational appraisal of the available evidence for that belief. It is easy to see how such a strategy could be useful to Jonas and Eva. Assessing the content of their beliefs, such as Jonas's belief that he needs Eva to stay with him at parties or that she should always organize the social calendar, or Eva's belief that Jonas should "get a grip and be more confident" or that he shouldn't go out with coworkers but stay home with her and the kids, could help both of them evaluate these beliefs and look for more objective alternatives. For example, if Jonas were to test his belief that he needed Eva at parties by experimenting with mingling on his own, he might come to recognize "It is nice when

Eva is with me, but I don't need her—I can enjoy mingling with others without her at my side." Likewise, if Eva came to believe "I would enjoy parties more if Jonas were better at being independent, but there is no law that says we can't stay together at parties," she might be less irritated and shift her perception that he is "clingy" to something more benign.

CBT interventions also represent change strategies that, from an ACT perspective, can be problematic. Koerner and colleagues (1994) point out that change strategies entail teaching new behaviors (including "cognitive" behaviors) for clients to utilize during stressful situations. Needing to employ a certain skill at so many junctures, sitting and doing problem solving to decide whose plan for Saturday night will be realized, or utilizing cognitive restructuring and doing a behavioral experiment to change their distressing beliefs about each other does not cover broader thematic problems Jonas and Eva experience. As Koerner and colleagues (1994) state, "the guiding principle of emotional acceptance work is to identify the contingencies of the couple's interaction pattern that are associated with pain, accusation, and blame across the content of their disagreements" (p. 113).

Cognitive Restructuring: An ACT/RFT View

Both cognitive behavioral couples therapy and enhanced cognitive behavioral couples therapy involve cognitive restructuring. Therapists within these traditions do not use cognitive restructuring exclusively or even primarily—this oversimplifies the approach. Nevertheless, there is an emphasis on cognitive restructuring within CBT approaches that is not found within

ACT. From an ACT/RFT perspective, cognitive restructuring can be beneficial in certain circumstances, but it can also be less than useful or even counterproductive.

Cognitive restructuring often involves changing thoughts to more accurately reflect reality. From an ACT perspective, noting what is coming to mind and questioning it is a useful enterprise. However, there is a subtle difference in how each therapy evaluates thoughts. Cognitive restructuring encourages a categorization of automatic thoughts (e.g., "all-or-nothing thinking") combined with an appreciation of their truthfulness or helpfulness. Clients are encouraged to examine the degree to which a particular thought is correct or incorrect. In addition, a cognitive behavioral therapist might ask clients to look at whether their thoughts are helpful or unhelpful, while maintaining that it may be beneficial to change the thought. In these circumstances, CBT is predominantly concerned with the *content* of thinking, as opposed to the context in which it occurs. In contrast, ACT addresses the context in which thoughts are held rigidly and literally. The goal is to alter the function of thoughts, building alternative responses to such private experiences. ACT is also concerned with thoughts' helpfulness (in accordance with the pragmatic truth criterion of functional contextualism), not their veracity. So, the question revolves not around what is true, but rather around how one relates to a particular thought.

In ACT, cognitive defusion de-emphasizes the thoughts themselves—whether they're accurate or not. One RFT-based distinction relevant to our understanding in this respect is that between Crel and Cfunc contextual control over relational framing. As explained in chapter 3, relational framing involves both derivation of relations and transformation of functions via those relations. RFT argues that both of these phenomena are under contextual control, and it uses the terms Crel and Cfunc, respectively, to refer to the cues that control each. So, for example, if you teach a child that "citronfärg means lemon," then the child might derive new relations of coordination or sameness between these two sounds as well as between "citronfärg" and the actual fruit. In this case, the word "means" is a Crel for deriving a relation of coordination between these stimuli. You might then ask the child some questions about a "citronfärg." You might first ask what it looks like and then ask what it tastes like. Even though the same newly verbal stimulus (i.e., "citronfärg") is involved, the child is likely to give different answers to these two questions—for example, "small, round, and yellow" in the first case and "sour" in the second. These different responses are controlled by the different Cfunc stimuli "look" and "taste," which result in different functions being transformed.

From an RFT point of view, there are Crel and Cfunc cues involved in all examples of relational framing, and manipulation of these cues controls the type of responding produced. RFT explains how cognitive restructuring contrasts with a typical ACT approach in terms of the type of cue manipulated as a response to potentially problematic behavior. Typically, cognitive restructuring involves an attempt to reduce the frequency of certain types of negative thoughts by making suggestions that are inconsistent with those thoughts. For example, if a client reports the thought *This relationship isn't working*, then the therapist may prompt the client to think of evidence countering that thought, such as ways in which the relationship *does* work. From an RFT perspective, this is classified as a Crel manipulation, because it involves trying to change the extent to which particular relations are derived.

However, RFT research provides evidence that relational networks are easier to elaborate than to reduce (e.g., Wilson & Hayes, 1996), which suggests that a Crel approach is more likely to work if the attempt at restructuring does not directly counteract the thought but instead coheres with it to at least some extent while allowing new, maximally helpful relations to be derived. An example of this would be for the therapist whose client reports the thought *This relationship isn't working* to agree that it seems as if the relationship is not working, and then ask the client whether this might be something that could be changed. Evidence (e.g., Clayton, 1995) suggests that this sort of approach might be more effective than prompting the client to think of evidence countering the thought.

In any event, however, ACT/RFT would suggest that Crel manipulations, in general, are potentially problematic for the reason that they tend to support patterns of transformation of functions via derived relational networks that are rigid, and thus in a broader context they can propagate problematic patterns of behavior. Hence, the preferred alternative, from an ACT/RFT perspective, is a Cfunc manipulation, in which control is exerted not over the extent to which relations are derived but over the extent to which functions in general are transformed via those relations. In a Cfunc manipulation, the therapist does not try to change the content of the relations that the client is deriving (e.g., "This relationship isn't working") but instead tries to change the client's response to that content so that he or she may continue to think such potentially problematic thoughts but not become "entangled" or "fused" with them. Thus, for example, the client can learn to respond to the thought

This relationship isn't working simply as a thought, as opposed to a true description of reality or a rule that must be followed.

Hence, from an ACT/RFT perspective, a Cfunc focused approach will tend to be more effective than a Crel focused one. One other thing to note at this point, however, is that even a Crel-focused approach can have elements that are somewhat conducive to facilitating Cfunc control, and may be effective to at least some extent for that reason. For example, even an approach that prompts a client to question particular thoughts might allow the client a certain distance from those thoughts and perhaps facilitate the client's seeing them as patterns of behavior in which he or she tends to engage rather than as immutable rules. Thus, some of the approaches that involve cognitive restructuring described here may to some extent facilitate more effective behavior in relation to problematic patterns of thinking. At the same time, of course, an approach like ACT that concentrates on facilitating such behavior—as opposed to simply providing conditions that might or might not support it—is likely to be more effective in counteracting fusion and inflexibility.

Returning to our case study, suppose that an ACT therapist decided to address Jonas's belief that he needs Eva to be with him at parties. Jonas initially might be encouraged to examine the consequences of having such a thought. He could easily recognize how the thought allows him to feel more comfortable when she is present. He could also articulate how he feels more anxious if she is not present, to the point where he is likely to avoid going to a party if she is not also going. Realizing that the effect of such thinking keeps him stuck in a bad place both socially and in terms if his relationship, Jonas would be encouraged to relate differently to the thought itself. Rather than generating a new thought (e.g., *I am fine being alone at parties*), he would be invited to experience this thought in a way that would make it silly or nonsensical. For example, he could sing "I need Eva tonight" to the tune of "Happy Birthday." The effect of such cognitive defusion strategies is to reduce the dominance of relational framing when it is not in the service of long-term goals or values. As an aside, it should be noted that cognitive behavioral approaches other than ACT (e.g., rational emotive behavior therapy, or REBT) incorporate strategies that can promote defusion; however, these approaches typically incorporate a mix of both cognitive restructuring and defusion-type strategies, and they tend to emphasize the first. More importantly, such approaches do not discriminate the effects of such strategies using a substantively analytic account of language processes, which is a primary advantage of an account based on ACT and working in tandem with RFT.

An Enhanced Cognitive Behavioral Therapy Perspective

Enhanced cognitive behavioral therapy for couples adds several components to "standard" CBT, including an appreciation of broader relationship themes, an interest in emotions (especially positive ones), an emphasis on environmental and contextual factors, and elicitation of partners' motives (Epstein & Baucom, 2002). An enhanced cognitive behavioral therapist might help Jonas and Eva articulate their particular needs or preferences or uncover their schematic beliefs by asking them a sequence of questions that reveal each partner's particular distress in various situations. As well as helping Eva and Jonas articulate beliefs as discussed previously from a CBT perspective, an enhanced CBT approach would consider the patterns of interaction that the couple have developed and help them discover or increase their acceptance of each other's personal characteristics and schemas. The therapist might use mini-lectures or readings, role-playing exercises, or cognitive strategies for modifying extreme or inflexible standards (Epstein & Baucom, 2002) to help Jonas and Eva see how their particular styles can be compatible.

ECBT Additions: An ACT/RFT View

From an ACT/RFT point of view, the helpfulness of additional elements provided by an ECBT approach in couples therapy depends on how they are treated or regarded. In the case of the interest in emotion, as has been explained previously in this book, ACT/RFT would suggest that if emotion, whether positive or negative, is simply seen as a natural behavior and not as something to be avoided, then this is a helpful conception. On the other hand, if ECBT advocates pursuing or maintaining particular emotions (e.g., positive ones) in some way while avoiding or regulating other emotions, then this is problematic.

An emphasis on environmental and contextual factors sits well with the contextualist underpinnings of ACT/RFT. From a behavioral point of view, environmental variables are key determinants of behavior and are therefore very relevant in any comprehensive psychological analysis, whether of individuals' behavior or couples'. ACT/RFT supplements such analyses with special types of contextualist analyses, including the idea that individuals can provide particular types of context (i.e., Cfunc) for their languaging behavior that are more or less helpful (with defusion and fusion as the respective outcomes of these different types of context) in achieving certain goals, including those pertinent in the context of a relationship.

From an ACT/RFT point of view, motives are a key part of a relationship analysis. Each partner's motives should, ultimately, be based on his or her chosen values. As we saw in chapters 4 and 7, in particular, chosen values are a critically important guide for behavior. In a successful relationship, both partners' values should include the health of the relationship itself; therefore, explicit discussion of motives for action as they relate to the overarching value of the relationship can be very beneficial. On the other hand, when contemplation or discussion of motives becomes divorced from the concept of valuing the relationship, and one or both partners become fused with alternative conceptions of motives (whether their own or their partner's), this is potentially problematic.

An Integrative Behavioral Couples Therapy (IBCT) Perspective

In IBCT, case formulation involves the identification of a theme (i.e., the couple's primary conflict), a polarization process (i.e., how the partners begin to draw apart in interactions), and a mutual trap (i.e., the outcome of conflicts). For Jonas and Eva, their primary conflict revolves around the theme of closeness versus distance. Eva wants to feel close to Jonas, and she experiences this closeness through everyday conversations and going out together. Jonas enjoys feeling close to Eva, though his needs are different. He feels connected to her through physical closeness and more intimate, "deeper" conversations. He enjoys when the two of them sit on the couch and watch TV. Meanwhile, to Eva, such experiences involve a "chasm" of silence between them. Conflict arises when they make efforts to feel closer to each other. For example, Eva might invite Jonas to go out to a party, which activates his social anxiety. Jonas, in turn, might be physically affectionate with Eva, which she rejects because she "doesn't feel close" to him. Ultimately, these conflicts lead to name-calling and giving up in frustration.

In order to help Jonas and Eva, an integrative behavioral couples therapist would use strategies to promote change, acceptance, and tolerance. One technique to promote emotional acceptance involves empathic joining around the problem. In this technique, a couple are invited to consider their difficulties as a shared problem, based on themes identified as part of the case formulation. To promote this realization, the therapist invites each partner to share his or her "softer" emotional experiences (sadness, fear, etc.) relative to their conflicts. When one partner expresses such vulnerability without any accompanying accusation or blame, it often prompts the other partner to respond in more loving ways. For example, Jonas and Eva would understand their difficulties as arising from the theme of closeness versus distance.

Emotional Acceptance: An ACT/RFT View

In IBCT, emotional acceptance changes the way in which partners relate to each other as well as to the underlying problem. Instead of pointing fingers, each partner comes to view the conflict as understandable, shared, and—in many cases—inevitable given their personal histories and behaviors. From an ACT/RFT perspective, emotional acceptance achieves this outcome by fundamentally altering the context in which conflict occurs. These changes happen both emotionally and cognitively.

The removal or reduction of blame during conflict creates a radical emotional shift in the experience of conflict for most couples. When feeling understood instead of attacked, partners are more likely to share and respond to each other's emotions empathically. There is less defensiveness and greater intimacy. The fundamental impasse may remain, but there is no blame laid. For example, Jonas and Eva might still get stuck in whether or not to go to a particular social function together. However, there would be less vitriol. In conversation, they both might express some sadness over the fact that they were having the same conflict again; Jonas might feel safe to share his fear of going out socially, while simultaneously acknowledging his guilt and shame in disappointing her. His expression of these softer feelings—as opposed to his criticizing Eva as "controlling" or "manipulative"—might in turn elicit more gentle responses from Eva.

In addition to the emotional piece, partners are invited to think about their difficulties from a different perspective. With the therapist's help in promoting a non-blaming understanding of their conflict, each partner will have a shared experience of "us as content" based on the primary theme. As long as this newly found understanding is held loosely, it can be quite helpful. For example, it would be helpful for Jonas and Eva to know that the basis of their mutual attraction (i.e., he loves her outgoingness and she loves his quieter introspection) occasionally becomes a source of conflict.

Summary

In this chapter, we explored the intersections between ACT/ RFT and several evidence-based behavioral and cognitive behavioral couples therapies. We provided a case example of Jonas and Eva, who were experiencing marital conflicts. We then provided a brief general ACT/RFT perspective on their difficulties, focusing on their fusion with thoughts about themselves and each other. Subsequently, we reviewed the couples therapies, exploring how each might work with Jonas and Eva. In the case of each approach, in turn, we described a particular intervention for Jonas and Eva that might be prescribed within that approach and then considered that intervention from an ACT/RFT perspective.

CHAPTER 10

Summary and Conclusions

Introduction

One of our main goals in writing this book has been to present a more scientific consideration of love than the popular view of love as an emotion. While we have not taken umbrage with the emotional aspects of love, and there is no denying that there are many "feel good" emotions associated with it, our basic premise has been that people who approach love as valued action may be less disappointed in their relationships than those who view and experience love primarily from the vantage point of emotion. We have approached this topic from the viewpoint of modern functional contextualist behavioral analysis and, more specifically, through the lenses of relational frame theory (RFT) and acceptance and commitment therapy (ACT). As a behavior analytic theory of human language and cognition, RFT affords an understanding of complex human behavior in the context of human relationships and explains and supports the kind of mid-level analysis of such behavior that ACT offers. The ACT/RFT analysis explains self-defeating patterns of behavior (e.g., fusion with unhelpful rules concerning the importance of particular emotions) while promoting alternative, beneficial behaviors (e.g., acting compassionately toward oneself and others and living in accordance with chosen values). The focus of this book has been on investigating and delineating both the former and the latter in the domain of romantic love.

Love is an important and beautiful aspect of human life. An intimate relationship can be a source of great joy as well as a source of great suffering and disappointment. By examining love in terms of RFT and ACT, we have offered a perspective that will, hopefully, promote the potential joy and vitality to be found in the domain of love while minimizing the pain and suffering that it can produce. We hope that our analysis will serve as a guide to researchers and clinicians as well as to individuals seeking deeper relationships.

Chapter 1: Mainstream Concepts of Love

In chapter 1, we referred to various researchers who looked at love from a number of different angles and from different theoretical positions. Mainstream psychological research has examined love as an emotion, looked at the neurological and biological aspects of love, explored love as both behavior and an evolutionary process, and considered the connotations of the word "love." And such scholarship has contributed much to our understanding of human love. Analysis of the complex series of behaviors, emotions, and cultural experiences that come together to make up the experience that we call "love" can certainly benefit from being comprehensively studied from many vantage points. At the same time, we point out that the predominant perspective of love in both academia and society at large highlights the emotional underpinning of love, which is potentially problematic. We proposed a useful alternative perspective from which to attempt to understand love, based in modern behavior analysis and RFT.

Chapters 2, 3, and 4: Basic Theory

Behavior analysis provides a science of human behavior that allows us to understand how complex behaviors occur and are established as operant processes. Behavior analysis itself is based on functional contextualist philosophical assumptions. From this perspective, all behavior can be considered as "action in context." People's experience of and understanding of love is a function of their individual learning histories, including the influence of their immediate socio-verbal environment as well as the cultural and collective learning histories that provide the larger context for their interpretations and experiences of human relationships. After introducing the philosophical assumptions underlying our approach in chapter 2, we discussed key behavioral concepts, including the operant or three-term contingency (ABC: antecedent—behavior—consequence) and generalization and discrimination learning. These concepts, which provide the basic scientific foundation for our approach, can serve to explain the earliest ontogenic origins of behavior in the context of relationships.

Traditional behavior analytic concepts by themselves are insufficient for understanding one key transformative aspect of human relationships: language. We approached the topic of language, and the influence of language on human relationships, using relational frame theory (RFT). RFT distinguishes the uniquely human ability to engage in arbitrarily applicable relational responding, also known as relational framing. As explained, this means relating objects and events under arbitrary contextual control, rather than on the basis of the physical properties of the things being related. There are many patterns of relational framing, which are referred to as "relational frames." They include sameness, distinction, opposition, analogical, and deictic (perspective-taking). All frames are characterized by three properties: (1) mutual entailment (i.e., a relation in one direction entails a relation in the other); (2) combinatorial entailment (i.e., two relations can combine to entail additional relations); and (3) transformation of stimulus functions (i.e., functions of stimuli that are relationally framed can change depending on the nature of the stimuli to which they are related and the nature of the relation). This third characteristic is critical from a psychological point of view, because it means that people's manner of responding to things can change rapidly, without direct "trial and error" training. For RFT, relational framing ability is the key to human language and can serve as the core explanation of many key phenomena relevant to human behavior—for example, psychopathology, perspective-taking, conceptualizations of self/other, and rule-governed behavior. In the last section of chapter 3, we provided a preliminary RFT analysis of the origins of romantic behavior, with some important guidelines for the use of RFT to interpret relationships.

Acceptance and commitment therapy (ACT), the subject of chapter 4, was explained as a response to the negative consequences of human language suggested by the RFT analysis in chapter 3. The key elements of ACT are acceptance of psychological events and commitment to values. From an ACT perspective, acceptance is a behavior. It involves being aware of and being willing to embrace private events. It represents also a willingness to accept reality as it is, not as how one would desire it to be, or construe it to be based on prior experiences. The ultimate goal of ACT is to help clients be psychologically flexible enough to accept what they need to accept in order to move in the direction of their values rather than remain fused with a conceptualized self (or other) that might prevent such movement. To promote flexibility, ACT guides contact with several complementary processes: acceptance and defusion, mindfulness and self-as-context, and values and committed action. Engagement with these processes can make clients psychologically healthier and, of key importance in the context of this book, more likely to engage in behavior supportive of intimacy.

We explained these processes before providing a preview of the ACT approach to relationships in the latter part of the chapter.

Chapters 5, 6, 7, and 8: ACT for Relationships

Chapters 5 through 8 examined problematic (chapters 5 and 6) and healthy (chapters 7 and 8) processes in relationships. The focus of chapter 5 was self-as-content and language traps. A key message in this book has been that establishing intimate relationships requires people to be open and vulnerable. In essence, intimate relationships require people to embrace potentially negative private experiences as they commit to valued actions toward their partner. Unfortunately, when people become fused with particular thoughts concerning themselves or their partner, they lose contact with potentially rewarding experiences in the relationship. These language traps can also occur around life roles, rules, and emotional experiences.

In chapter 6, we looked at the issue of rigidity in relationships. One fundamental obstacle to intimacy in relationships occurs when people habitually avoid particular kinds of private experiences or events. In efforts to not experience pain, fear, or rejection, people can develop patterns of behavior that interfere with their ability to connect to others openly and intimately. Thus, such rigidity garners short-term avoidance of particular types of experience at the expense of living in accordance with one's innermost values.

In chapter 7, we considered valuing. We emphasized that values should not be seen as feelings and that, while positive feelings may be a consequence of acting in a valued fashion (because to do so is inherently reinforcing), pursuing happiness or other positive feelings as ends in themselves often results in exactly the opposite. Such a pursuit can take people away from the present moment, effectively putting their life on hold until they attain the desired feeling. In intimate relationships, attempts to avoid vulnerability and negative experiences or looking to be constantly reinforced by one's partner can be particularly destructive. Psychological flexibility is particularly important in this area, because rigidity in trying to control or limit one's own pain can result in acting in ways that are inconsistent with one's values.

In chapter 8, we explored the concept of self-compassion. It has been our contention that looking at relationships from an RFT perspective, and applying the principles put forward in ACT, can help people attain vital intimate relationships. Based on an RFT explanation of empathy and the verbal other, self-compassion is a key step in enabling people to extend kindness and love toward another person. Hence, as explained in this chapter, self-compassion can provide an important foundation for the development of a loving intimate relationship.

Chapter 9: Therapy and Relationships

In chapter 9, we examined several therapies that have been carefully researched and that have demonstrated efficacy in helping distressed couples improve their relationships. These therapies, while they differ from ACT in specific applications, can be considered from the vantage point of RFT. Integrative behavioral couples therapy and enhanced cognitive behavioral therapy for

251

couples share goals espoused by ACT: to help couples shift the context, rather than just the content, of their interactions, embracing conflict as a part of relationships and working toward greater understanding and acceptance of each other. This requires compassion for one's partner, as well as compassion for oneself. The willingness to embrace private experiences, especially negative private experiences, requires people to be aware of their evaluations of themselves and others, and to observe, but not become fused with, those evaluations.

Conclusion

It is safe to say that like many people, we love to love. Loving is a natural, vital part of being human, and we embrace many varieties of the experience of love and intimacy. However, it has been our contention that the modern emphasis on romantic love (particularly in the Western world) has contributed to much dissatisfaction and disillusionment. In this book, we have offered an alternative perspective. By seeing love as valued action, rather than as a psychological state that one "falls into" or "falls out of," people can commit themselves to being loving partners, friends, and relatives. Particularly in intimate relationships, they can work to sustain deeply meaningful and intimate connections over the course of time, embracing the inevitable disappointments and lows as well as the joys and highs. People can remain committed to their partner even when he or she doesn't live up to expectations or isn't true to their conception. They can have compassion for themselves, defuse from their conceptualized selves, and accept reality as it is. Relationships exist in the "here and now," and people do not need to be trapped and prevented from enjoying the beauty of this present experience by hurts from the past or fears of the future. With a focus on the present, people may experience suffering, but they can also experience good feelings as a consequence of valued action. They can also find someone special with whom to share a vital and fulfilled life, one that can sometimes take them to proverbial mountaintops and at other times into deep caverns. Throughout human history, sharing one's experience of life with another has been powerfully reinforcing. With this book, we hope that you have considered new possibilities for improving and maintaining this highly valued human experience.

References

Abramowitz, J. S., Tolin, D. F., & Street, G. P. (2001). Paradoxical effects of thought suppression: A meta-analysis of controlled studies. *Clinical Psychology Review, 21*(5), 683–703.

Acevedo, B. P., & Aron, A. (2009). Does a long-term relationship kill romantic love? *Review of General Psychology, 13*(1), 59–65.

Acevedo, B. P., Aron, A., Fisher, H. E., & Brown, L. L. (2012). Neural correlates of long-term intense romantic love. *Social Cognitive and Affective Neuroscience, 7*(2), 145–159.

Acker, M., & Davis, M. (1992). Intimacy, passion and commitment in adult romantic relationships: A test of the triangular theory of love. *Journal of Social and Personal Relationships, 9*(1), 21–50.

Aron, A., Fisher, H., Mashek, D. J., Strong, G., Li, H., & Brown, L. L. (2005). Reward, motivation, and emotion systems associated with early-stage intense romantic love. *Journal of Neurophysiology, 94*(1), 327–337.

Aron, A., & Westbay, L. (1996). Dimensions of the prototype of love. *Journal of Personality and Social Psychology, 70*(3), 535–551.

Ayllon, T., & Azrin, N. H. (1964). Reinforcement and instructions with mental patients. *Journal of the Experimental Analysis of Behavior, 7*(4), 327–331.

Baer, D. M., Peterson, R. F., & Sherman, J. A. (1967). The development of imitation by reinforcing behavioral similarity to a model. *Journal of the Experimental Analysis of Behavior, 10*(5), 405–416.

Bandura, A. (1977). *Social learning theory* (2nd ed.). Englewood Cliffs, NJ: Prentice Hall.

Barnes-Holmes, D., Hayes, S. C., & Dymond, S. (2001). Self and self-directed rules. In S. C. Hayes, D. Barnes-Holmes, & B. Roche (Eds.), *Relational frame theory: A post-Skinnerian account of human language and cognition.* New York: Plenum.

Barnes-Holmes, Y., Barnes-Holmes, D., & Smeets, P. M. (2004). Establishing relational responding in accordance with opposite as generalized operant behavior in young children. *International Journal of Psychology and Psychological Therapy, 4*(3), 559–586.

Barnes-Holmes, Y., Barnes-Holmes, D., Smeets, P. M., Strand, P., & Friman, P. (2004). Establishing relational responding in accordance with more-than and less-than as generalized operant behavior in young children. *International Journal of Psychology and Psychological Therapy, 4*(3), 531–558.

Baron, A., Kaufman, A., & Stauber, K. A. (1969). Effects of instructions and reinforcement-feedback on human operant behavior maintained by fixed-interval reinforcement. *Journal of the Experimental Analysis of Behavior, 12,* 701–712.

Beck, J. G., Bozman, A. W., & Qualtrough, T. (1991). The experience of sexual desire: Psychological correlates in a college sample. *Journal of Sex Research, 28*(3), 443–456.

Berens, N. M., & Hayes, S. C. (2007). Arbitrarily applicable comparative relations: Experimental evidence for relational operants. *Journal of Applied Behavior Analysis, 40,* 45–71.

Blackledge, J. T. (2007). Disrupting verbal processes: Cognitive defusion in acceptance and commitment therapy and other mindfulness-based psychotherapies. *The Psychological Record, 57*(4), 555–577.

Blackledge, J. T., & Barnes-Holmes, D. (2009). Core processes in acceptance and commitment therapy. In J. T. Blackledge, J. Ciarrochi, & F. P. Deane (Eds.), *Acceptance and commitment therapy: Contemporary theory, research and practice* (pp. 41–58). Bowen Hills, QLD, Australia: Australian Academic Press.

Block, J. (1979). Another look at sex differentiation in the socialization behaviors of mothers and fathers. In F. Denmark & J. Sherman (Eds.), *Psychology of women: Future directions of research.* New York: Psychological Dimensions.

Buckley, K. W. (1994). Misbehaviorism: The case of John B. Watson's dismissal from Johns Hopkins University. In J. T. Todd & E. K. Morris (Eds.), *Modern perspectives on John B. Watson and classical behaviorism.* Westwood, CT: Greenwood Press.

Buss, D. M. (2006). The evolution of love. In R. J. Sternberg & K. Weis (Eds.), *The new psychology of love*. New Haven, CT: Yale University Press.

Cacioppo, J. T., Hughes, M. E., Waite, L. J., Hawkley, L. C., & Thisted, R. A. (2006). Loneliness as a specific risk factor for depressive symptoms: Cross-sectional and longitudinal analyses. *Psychology and Aging*, 21(1), 140–151.

Cacioppo, S., Bianchi-Demicheli, F., Hatfield, E., & Rapson, R. L. (2012). Social neuroscience of love. *Clinical Neuropsychiatry: Journal of Treatment Evaluation*, 9(1), 3–13.

Carpentier, F., Smeets, P. M., & Barnes-Holmes, D. (2003). Equivalence-equivalence as a model of analogy: Further analyses. *The Psychological Record*, 53, 349–372.

Cassepp-Borges, V., & Pasquali, L. (2012). Sternberg's Triangular Love Scale National Study of Psychometric Attributes. *Paidéia*, 22(51), 21–31.

Christensen, A., Atkins, D. C., Baucom, D. H., & Yi, J. (2010). Marital status and satisfaction five years following a randomized clinical trial comparing traditional versus integrative behavioral couple therapy. *Journal of Consulting and Clinical Psychology*, 74, 1180–1191.

Christensen, A., Atkins, D. C., Bern, S., Wheeler, J., Baucom, D. H., & Simpson, L. E. (2004). Traditional versus integrative behavioral couple therapy for significantly and chronically distressed married couples. *Journal of Consulting and Clinical Psychology*, 72, 176–191.

Christensen, A., Atkins, D. C., Yi, J., Baucom, D. H., & George, W. H. (2006). Couple and individual adjustment for two years following a randomized clinical trial comparing traditional versus integrative behavioral couple therapy. *Journal of Consulting and Clinical Psychology*, 78, 225–235.

Christensen, A., & Heavey, C. L. (1999). Interventions for couples. *Annual Review of Psychology*, 50, 165–190.

Clayton, T. M. (1995). Changing organizational culture through relational framing. Masters' thesis available from the University of Nevada, Reno.

Coontz, S. (1992). *The way we never were: American families and the nostalgia trap*. New York: Basic Books.

Coontz, S. (2005). *Marriage, a history: From obedience to intimacy or how love conquered marriage*. New York: Viking.

Dahl, J. C., Plumb, J. C., Stewart, I., & Lundgren, T. (2009). *The art and science of valuing in psychotherapy: Helping clients discover, explore, and commit to valued action using acceptance and commitment therapy.* Oakland, CA: New Harbinger Publications.

Damon, W., & Hart, D. (1988). *Self-understanding in childhood and adolescence.* Cambridge: Cambridge University Press.

Diener, E. (2000). Subjective well-being. The science of happiness and a proposal for a national index. *American Psychologist, 55*(1), 34–43.

Dymond, S., May, R. J., Munnelly, A., & Hoon, A. E. (2010). Evaluating the evidence base for relational frame theory: A citation analysis. *The Behavior Analyst, 33,* 97–117.

Dymond, S., & Roche, B. (Eds.). (2013). *Advances in relational frame theory: Research and application.* Oakland, CA: New Harbinger Publications.

Epstein, N. B., & Baucom, D. H. (2002). *Enhanced cognitive-behavioral therapy for couples: A contextual approach.* Washington, DC: American Psychological Association.

Farroni, T., Csibra, G., Simion, F., & Johnson, M. H. (2002). Eye contact detection in humans from birth. *Proceedings of National Academy of Science* (USA), *99,* 9602–9605.

Fehr, B. (1988). Prototype analysis of the concepts of love and commitment. *Journal of Personality and Social Psychology, 55*(4), 557–579.

Fisher, H., Aron, A., & Brown, L. L. (2005). Romantic love: An fMRI study of a neural mechanism for mate choice. *Journal of Comparative Neurology, 493,* 58–62.

Fisher, H. E., Aron, A., & Brown, L. L. (2006). Romantic love: A mammalian brain system for mate choice. *Philosophical Transactions of the Royal Society B, 361,* 2173–2186.

Gilbert, D. (2007). *Stumbling on happiness.* New York: Vintage.

Giurfa, M., Zhang, S., Jenett, A., Menzel, R., & Srinivasan, M. V. (2011). The concepts of sameness and difference in an insect. *Nature, 410,* 930–932.

Gonzaga, G. C., Turner, R. A., Keltner, D., Campos, B., & Altemus, M. (2006). Romantic love and sexual desire in close relationships. *Emotion, 6*(2), 163–179.

Gottman, J., & Silver, N. (2000). *The seven principles for making marriage work: A practical guide from the country's foremost relationship expert.* New York: Three Rivers Press.

Gottman, J. M., Levenson, R. W., Swanson, C., Swanson, K., Tyson, R., & Yoshimoto, D. (2003). Observing gay, lesbian, and heterosexual couples' relationships: Mathematical modeling of conflict interaction. *Journal of Homosexuality, 45*, 65–91.

Harlow, H. F., & Zimmermann, R. R. (1958). The development of affective responsiveness in infant monkeys. *Proceedings of the American Philosophical Society, 102*, 501–509.

Hatfield, E. (2006, Spring). The Golden Fleece Award. Relationship Research News. New York: International Academy of Relationship Research.

Hatfield, E., & Rapson, R. L. (2006). Passionate love, sexual desire, and mate selection: Cross-cultural and historical perspectives. In E. Hatfield & R. L. Rapson (Eds.), *Close relationships: Functions, forms and processes* (pp. 227–243). Hove, England: Psychology Press/Taylor & Francis (UK).

Hatfield, E., Traupmann, J., & Sprecher, S. (1984). Older women's perceptions of their intimate relationships. *Journal of Social and Clinical Psychology, 2*(2), 108–124.

Hatfield, E., & Walster, G. W. (1978). *A new look at love: A revealing report on the most elusive of all emotions.* Lanham, MD: University Press of America.

Hayes, S., Bissett, R., Roget, N., Padilla, M., Kohlenberg, B., Fisher, G., et al. (2004). The impact of Acceptance and Commitment Training and multicultural training on the stigmatizing attitudes and professional burnout of substance abuse counselors. *Behavior Therapy, 35*, 821–835.

Hayes, S. C. (1984). Making sense of spirituality. *Behaviorism, 12*, 99–110.

Hayes, S. C. (1989). *Rule-governed behavior: Cognition, contingencies, and instructional control.* New York: Plenum Press.

Hayes, S. C. (1994). Content, context, and the types of psychological acceptance. In S. C. Hayes, N. S. Jacobson, V. M. Follette, & M. J. Dougher (Eds.), *Acceptance and change: Content and context in psychotherapy.* Reno, NV: Context Press.

Hayes, S. C. (1995). The role of cognition in complex human behavior: A contextualistic perspective. *Journal of Behavior Therapy and Experimental Psychiatry, 26*(3), 241–248.

Hayes, S. C. (2008). *The roots of compassion.* Keynote speech delivered at the International ACT Conference, Chicago.

Hayes, S. C., Barnes-Holmes, D., & Roche, B. (Eds.). (2001). *Relational frame theory: A post-Skinnerian account of human language and cognition*. New York: Kluwer Academic/Plenum.

Hayes, S. C., Brownstein, A. J., Haas, J. R., & Greenway, D. E. (1986). Instructions, multiple schedules and extinction: Distinguishing rule-governed from schedule-controlled behavior. *Journal of the Experimental Analysis of Behavior, 46*, 137–147.

Hayes, S. C., Hayes, L. J., & Reese, H. W. (1988). Finding the philosophical core: A review of Stephen C. Pepper's *World Hypotheses. Journal of the Experimental Analysis of Behavior, 50*, 97–111.

Hayes, S. C., Strosahl, K. D., & Wilson, K. G. (1999). *Acceptance and commitment therapy: An experiential approach to behavior change*. New York: Guilford Press.

Hayes, S. C., Wilson, K. W., Gifford, E. V., Follette, V. M., & Strosahl, K. (1996). Experiential avoidance and behavioral disorders: A functional dimensional approach to diagnosis and treatment. *Journal of Consulting and Clinical Psychology, 64*(6), 1152–1168.

Holmes, T. H., & Rahe, R. H. (1967). The social readjustment rating scale. *Journal of Psychosomatic Research, 11*(2), 213–218.

Jacobson, N. S., & Christensen, A. (1998). *Acceptance and change in couple therapy: A therapist's guide to transforming relationships*. New York: Norton.

Jacobson, N. S., Follette, W. C., Revenstorf, D., Baucom, D. H., Halweg, K., & Margolin, G. (1984). Variability in outcome and clinical significance of behavioral marital therapy: A reanalysis of outcome date. *Journal of Consulting and Clinical Psychology, 52*, 497–501.

Jacobson, N. S., & Margolin, G. (1979). *Marital therapy: Strategies based on social learning and behavior exchange principles*. New York: Brunner/Mazel.

Kaufman, A., Baron, A., & Kopp, R. E. (1966). Some effects of instructions on human operant behavior. *Psychonomic Monograph Supplements, 1*, 243–250.

Koerner, K., Jacobson, N. S., & Christensen, A. (1994). Emotional acceptance in integrative behavioral couple therapy. In S. Hayes, N. S. Jacobson, V. M. Follette, & M. J. Dougher (Eds.), *Acceptance and change: Content and context in psychotherapy*. Reno, NV: Context Press.

Kross, E., Berman, M. G., Mischel, W., Smith, E. E., & Wager, T. D. (2011). Social rejection shares somatosensory representations with physical pain. *Proceedings of the National Academy of Sciences, USA, 108,* 6270–6275.

Kurdek, L. A. (1998). Relationship outcomes and their predictors: Longitudinal evidence from heterosexual married, gay cohabiting, and lesbian cohabiting couples. *Journal of Marriage and the Family, 60,* 553–568.

Kurdek, L. A. (2004). Gay men and lesbians: The family context. In M. Coleman & L. H. Ganong (Eds.), *Handbook of contemporary families: Considering the past, contemplating the future* (pp. 96–115). Newbury Park, CA: Sage.

Kurdek, L. A. (2005). What do we know about gay and lesbian couples? *Current Directions in Psychological Science, 14*(5), 251–254.

Landis, D., & O'Shea III, W. A. (2000). Cross-cultural aspects of passionate love: An individual differences analysis. *Journal of Cross-Cultural Psychology, 31,* 752–777.

Lao-tzu. (n.d.). Love is of all passions the strongest, for it attacks simultaneously the head, the heart... - Lao Tzu at Brainy Quote. Retrieved from http://www.brainyquote.com/quotes/quotes/l/laotzu387058.html

Lee, J. A. (1977). A topology of styles of loving. *Personality and Social Psychology Bulletin, 3,* 173–182.

Lee, T. M. C., Leung, M.-K., Hou, W.-K., Tang, J. C. Y., Yin, J., So, K.-F.,...Chan, C. C. H. (2012). Distinct neural activity associated with focused-attention meditation and loving-kindness meditation. *PLoS ONE, 7*(8), e40054. doi:10.1371/journal.pone.0040054

Lillis, J., Luoma, J., Levin, M., & Hayes, S. (2010). Measuring weight self-stigma: The weight self-stigma questionnaire. *Obesity, 18,* 971–976.

Luoma, J., O'Hair, A., Kohlenberg, B., Hayes, S., & Fletcher, L. (2010). The development and psychometric properties of a new measure of perceived stigma towards substance users. *Substance Use and Misuse, 45,* 47–57.

Luoma, J. B., Hayes, S. C., Twohig, M. P., Roget, N., Fisher, G., Padilla, M.,...Kohlenberg, B. (2007). Augmenting continuing education with psychologically focused group consultation: Effects on adoption of group drug counseling. *Psychotherapy: Theory, Research, Practice, Training, 44*(4), 463–469.

Lutz, A., Brefczynski-Lewis, J., Johnstone, T., & Davidson, R. J. (2008). Regulation of the neural circuitry of emotion by compassion meditation: Effects of meditative expertise. *PLoS ONE*, 3(3), e1897. doi:10.1371/journal.pone.0001897

Masuda, A., Hayes, S. C., Fletcher, L. B., Seignourel, P. J., Bunting, K., Herbst, S. A., Twohig, M. P., & Lillis, J. (2007). Impact of acceptance and commitment therapy versus education on stigma toward people with psychological disorders. *Behavior Research and Therapy*, 45, 2764–2772.

Masuda, A., Hayes, S., Lillis, J., Bunting, K., Herbst, S., & Fletcher, L. (2009). The relationship between psychological flexibility and mental health stigma in acceptance and commitment therapy: A preliminary process investigation. *Behavior and Social Issues*, 18, 25–40.

Matthews, B. A., Shimoff, E., Catania, A. C., & Sagvolden, T. (1977). Uninstructed human responding: Sensitivity to ration and interval contingencies. *Journal of the Experimental Analysis of Behavior*, 27, 453–467.

Mauss, I. B., Savino, N. S., Anderson, C. L., Weisbuch, M., Tamir, M., & Laudenslager, M. L. (2012). The pursuit of happiness can be lonely. *Emotion*, 12(5), 908–912.

Mauss, I. B., Tamir, M., Anderson, C. L., & Savino, N. S. (2011). Can seeking happiness make people unhappy? Paradoxical effects of valuing happiness. *Emotion*, 11, 807–815.

McHugh, L., Barnes-Holmes, Y., & Barnes-Holmes, B. (2004). Perspective-taking as relational responding: A developmental profile. *The Psychological Record*, 54(1), 115–144.

McHugh, L., Barnes-Holmes, Y., Barnes-Holmes, D., & Stewart, I. (2006). Understanding false belief as generalized operant behavior. *The Psychological Record*, 56, 341–364.

Meyers, S. A., & Berscheid, E. (1997). The language of love: The difference a preposition makes. *Personality and Social Psychology Bulletin*, 23(4), 347–362.

Michael, J. (1982). Distinguishing between discriminative and motivational functions of stimuli. *Journal of the Experimental Analysis of Behavior*, 37(1), 149–155.

Myers, D. G. (2000). The funds, friends, and faith of happy people. *American Psychologist*, 55(1), 56–67.

Neff, K. (2003). Self-compassion: An alternative conceptualization of a healthy attitude towards oneself. *Self and Identity, 2,* 85–102.

Neff, K., & Beretvas, S. N. (2012). The role of self-compassion in romantic relationships, self and identity. doi:10.1080/15298868.2011.639548

O'Leary, K. D., Acevedo, B. P., Aron, A., Huddy, L., & Mashek, D. (2012). Is long-term love more than a rare phenomenon? If so, what are its correlates? *Social Psychological and Personality Science, 3*(2), 241–249.

Ortigue, S., Bianchi-Demicheli, F., Patel, N., Frum, C., & Lewis, J. W. (2010). Neuroimaging of love: fMRI meta-analysis evidence toward new perspectives in sexual medicine. *Journal of Sexual Medicine, 7,* 3541–3552.

Parker-Pope, T. (2010). *For better: The science of a good marriage.* New York: Dutton.

Pepper, S. C. (1942). *World hypotheses: A study in evidence.* Berkeley: University of California Press.

Regan, P. C. (2000). The role of sexual desire and sexual activity in dating relationships. *Social Behavior and Personality, 28*(1), 51–59.

Rehfeldt, R. A., & Barnes-Holmes, Y. (Eds.). (2009). *Derived relational responding: Applications for learners with autism and other developmental disabilities.* Oakland, CA: Context Press/New Harbinger Publications.

Robinson, P. J., Gould, D., & Strosahl, K. D. (2011). *Real behavior change in primary care: Strategies and tools for improving outcomes and increasing job satisfaction.* Oakland, CA: New Harbinger Publications.

Roche, B., & Barnes, D. (1997). A transformation of respondently conditioned stimulus function in accordance with arbitrarily applicable relations. *Journal of the Experimental Analysis of Behavior, 67,* 275–300.

Rosales, R., Rehfeldt, R. A., & Lovett, S. (2011). Effects of multiple exemplar training on the emergence of derived relations in preschool children learning a second language. *The Analysis of Verbal Behavior, 27,* 61–74.

Schnarch, D. (2011). *Intimacy and desire: Awaken the passion in your relationship.* New York: Beaufort Books.

Schneiderman, I., Zagoory-Sharon, O., Leckman, J. F., & Feldman, R. (2012). Oxytocin during the initial stages of romantic attachment: Relations to couples' interactive reciprocity. *Psychoneuroendocrinology, 37,* 1277–1285.

Schoenfeld, E. A., Bredow, C. A., & Huston, T. L. (2012). Do men and women show love differently in marriage? *Personality and Social Psychology Bulletin*, 38(11), 1396–1409.

Schooler, J. W., Ariely, D., & Loewenstein, G. (2003). The pursuit and assessment of happiness may be self-defeating. In J. Carrillo & I. Brocas (Eds.), *The psychology of economic decisions* (pp. 41–70). Oxford: Oxford University Press.

Shadish, W. R., & Baldwin, S. A. (2003). Meta-analysis of marital family therapy interventions. *Journal of Marital and Family Therapy, 29*, 547–570.

Shadish, W. R., & Baldwin, S. A. (2005). Effects of behavioral marital therapy: A meta-analysis of randomized controlled trials. *Journal of Consulting and Clinical Psychology, 73*, 6–14.

Shadish, W. R., Montgomery, L. M., Wilson, P., Wilson, M. R., Bright, I., & Okwumabua, T. (1993). Effects of family and marital psychotherapies: A meta-analysis. *Journal of Consulting and Clinical Psychology, 61*, 992–1002.

Shimoff, E., Catania, A. C., & Matthews, B. A. (1981). Uninstructed human responding: Sensitivity of low rate human performances to schedule contingencies. *Journal of the Experimental Analysis of Behavior, 36*, 207–220.

Skinner, B. F. (1957). *Verbal behavior.* New York: Appleton-Century-Crofts.

Skinner, B. F. (1966). An operant analysis of problem solving. In B. Kleinmuntz (Ed.), *Problem solving: Research, method and theory* (pp. 133–171). New York: John Wiley & Sons.

Skinner, B. F. (1971). *Beyond freedom and dignity.* New York: Knopf.

Skinner, B. F. (1974). *About behaviorism.* New York: Alfred Knopf.

Skinner, B. F. (1989). *The origins of cognitive thought.* Recent Issues in the Analysis of Behavior, Merrill Publishing.

Snyder, D. K., Castellani, A.M., & Whisman, M. A. (2006). Current status and future directions in couple therapy. *Annual Review of Psychology, 57*, 317–344.

Sprecher, S., & Fehr, B. (2011). Dispositional attachment and relationship-specific attachment as predictors of compassionate love for a partner. *Journal of Social and Personal Relationships, 28*(4), 558–574.

Steele, D. L., & Hayes, S. C. (1991). Stimulus equivalence and arbitrarily applicable relational responding. *Journal of the Experimental Analysis of Behavior,* 56, 519–555.

Sternberg, R. (1997). Construct validation of a triangular love scale. *European Journal of Social Psychology,* 27, 313–335.

Sternberg, R. J. (1986). A triangular theory of love. *Psychological Review,* 93, 119–135.

Steverink, N., & Lindenberg, S. (2006). Which social needs are important for subjective well being? What happens to them with aging? *Psychology and Aging,* 21(2), 281–290.

Stewart, I., Barnes-Holmes, D., & Roche, B. (2004). A functional analytic model of analogy using the Relational Evaluation Procedure. *The Psychological Record,* 54(4), 531–552.

Sulzer-Azaroff, B., & Mayer, G. R. (1991). *Behavior analysis for lasting change.* Belmont, CA: Wadsworth Publishing.

Uchida, Y., Norasakkunkit, V., & Kitayama, S. (2004). Cultural constructions of happiness: Theory and empirical evidence. *Journal of Happiness Studies,* 5, 223–239. doi:10.1007/s 10902-004-8785-9

Underwood, L. G. (2008). Compassionate love: A framework for research. In B. Fehr, S. Sprecher, & L. G. Underwood (Eds.), *The science of compassionate love: Theory, research, and applications.* Malden, MA: Wiley-Blackwell.

Watts, S., & Stenner, P. (2005). The subjective experience of partnership love: A Q methodological study. *British Journal of Social Psychology,* 44, 85–107.

Weiner, H. (1970). Instructional control of human operant responding during extinction following fixed-ratio conditioning. *Journal of the Experimental Analysis of Behavior,* 13, 391–394.

Wilson, K. G., & Dufrene, T. (2009). *Mindfulness for two: An acceptance and commitment therapy approach to mindfulness in psychotherapy.* Oakland, CA: New Harbinger Publications.

Wilson, K. G., & Hayes, S. C. (1996). Resurgence of derived stimulus relations. *Journal of the Experimental Analysis of Behavior,* 66(3), 267–281.

Wood, N. D., Crane, D. R., Schaalje, G. B., & Law, D. D. (2005). What works for whom: A meta-analytic review of marital and couples therapy in reference to marital distress. *The American Journal of Family Therapy,* 33, 273–287.

Xu, X., Wang, J., Aron, A., Lei, W., Westmaas, J. L., & Weng, X. (2012). Intense passionate love attenuates cigarette cue-reactivity in nicotine-deprived smokers: An fMRI study. *PLoS ONE, 7*(7), e42235. doi:10.1371/journal.pone.0042235

Yadavaia, J. E., & Hayes, S. C. (2012). Acceptance and commitment therapy for self-stigma around sexual orientation: A multiple baseline evaluation. *Cognitive and Behavioral Practice, 19*(4), 545–559.

Yarnell, L. M., and Neff, K. D. (2013). Self-compassion, interpersonal conflict resolutions, and well-being. *Self and Identity, 12*(2), 146–159.

Zettle, R. D., & Hayes, S. C. (1982). Rule governed behavior: A potential theoretical framework for cognitive-behavior therapy. In P. C. Kendall (Ed.), *Advances in cognitive-behavioral research and therapy* (Vol. 1, pp. 73–118). New York: Academic.

JoAnne Dahl, PhD, is professor of psychology at Uppsala University, Sweden. She is coauthor of *Living Beyond Your Pain, The Art and Science of Valuing in Psychotherapy,* and *Acceptance and Commitment Therapy for Chronic Pain.* Dahl hosts a weekly radio program on ACT, and specializes in creating ACT applications for chronic illness, as well as those suffering in the developing countries.

Ian Stewart, PhD, is a faculty member in the school of psychology at the National University of Ireland, Galway, and coauthor of *The Art and Science of Valuing in Psychotherapy.*

Christopher Martell, PhD, is clinical associate professor of psychology at the University of Wisconsin-Milwaukee and a clinical research consultant. He is coauthor of *Overcoming Depression One Step at a Time.*

Jonathan S. Kaplan, PhD, is a clinical psychologist, adjunct professor, and author of *Urban Mindfulness: Cultivating Peace, Purpose, and Presence in the Middle of It All.* He has been incorporating mindfulness and meditation into psychotherapy for the past fifteen years. His work has been featured in *O, The Oprah Magazine,* as well as on the BBC News, MSNBC, and on radio and TV stations across the United States. He maintains a private practice in New York City.

Foreword writer **Robyn D. Walser, PhD,** is the assistant director at the National Center for PTSD at the Veterans Affairs Palo Alto Health Care System. She also works as a consultant, workshop presenter, and therapist in her private business, TLConsultation Services. She has facilitated ACT training workshops across the world since 1998.

Index

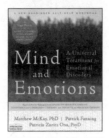

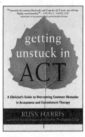